# FINDING LEONARDO

## THE CASE FOR RECOVERING
## THE BATTLE OF ANGHIARI

**Rab Hatfield**

Cover and book design: Marco Badiani, agilelogica.it
Layout: Cathy Gale, for agilelogica.it
Copyediting and proofreading: Ellen Wert, for The Florentine Press

Cover: Leonardo da Vinci, *Head of a Warrior*, 1504–5, Budapest Museum
Cover art and illustrations on pages 55 and 57–62 by permission
of Archivio Alinari Firenze and the Bridgeman Art Library - Archivio
Alinari Firenze.
Illustration on p. 56 courtesy of Maurizio Seracini.

ISBN 978-88-902434-1-7
1º edizione: dicembre 2007
2007 B'Gruppo srl, Prato
Collana The Florentine Press
Riproduzione vietata

1st edition: December 2007
All rights reserved
© Rab Hatfield

Richard C. Trexler

*in memoriam*

# THE FRIENDS OF FLORENCE FOUNDATION

The great reawakening of the human spirit that began in Florence in the twelfth century decreed the end of the Middle Ages. The study of antiquity—the glory of Ancient Greece, the grandeur of Rome—became a Florentine passion. Along with this passion there was a new impetus in research, scholarship and a new approach to creativity. It was precisely this blossoming of Florentine creativity that made the city the center of western civilization for art and letters, architecture and philosophy, the sciences and political idealism. The small city of Florence became the symbol of humanism and gave the world the great minds of Giotto, Dante Alighieri, Boccaccio, Leonardo da Vinci, Michelangelo, Brunelleschi, Galileo Galilei, Machiavelli, Marsilio Ficino and many other creators of artworks and ideals that continue to inspire the world even today.

Now, at the beginning of the third millennium, it is more important than ever that the cultural heritage of Florence and Tuscany be conserved, enhanced when possible and protected. The city of Florence is a work of art in itself, rich in palazzos, museums, hidden corners and splendid gardens: treasures that must be carefully protected and preserved for centuries to come since they are symbols of humanism, creativity and human genius. Unfortunately, many of the unique treasures that are in Florence and Tuscany risk ruin due to neglect or sporadic conservation.

It is for this reason that the international foundation Friends of Florence was born. It is a non-profit organization with headquarters in the United States of America. It was created and is supported by people from all over the world and is dedicated to conserving and enhancing the historical-cultural integrity of the city and its surroundings. Many artistic and architectural treasures will be restored, protected and made finally visible to the public through carefully planned and selected projects.

Furthermore, Friends of Florence is devoted to the divulgation and study of artworks in Tuscany—and in Florence in particular—through educational programs and activities. Every year the members have the opportunity to savor the glories of this magnificent city through special educational programs conducted by experts in the arts, historical-artistic conservation, architecture and other fields. Furthermore, they also have the privilege of visiting private collections that are generally not open to the public and of observing restoration projects launched by the Friends of Florence and other leading institutions, thereby becoming real 'citizens' of Florence.

Friends of Florence
www.friendsofflorence.org
info@friendsofflorence.org

4545 W Street N.W.
Washington DC 20007 USA

Via Ugo Foscolo 72
Florence 50124 Italy

# TABLE OF CONTENTS

# LIST OF ILLUSTRATIONS

# PREFACE

This book about recovering Leonardo da Vinci's *Capture of a Standard* originated as a long article to be submitted to the *Journal of the Warburg and Courtauld Institutes* (London). That fact explains the book's scholarly tone, the spelling and various editorial conventions.

But in the spring of 2007 a fortunate circumstance made me change my plans: Francesco Rutelli, vice president of Italy, ordered that a new search be made for Leonardo's great painting (a previous search had been conducted in the late 1970s). Rutelli also ordered that a commission be formed to supervise the search. I am a member of this commission. The search, scheduled to begin in September 2008, will be conducted by Maurizio Seracini.

As the publication times of scholarly periodicals can be several months or even years, I realized that a faster means of publication would now be necessary. Who, after all, wants to read an article predicting where Leonardo's painting might be found after the painting already *has* been found—or, if that is how things turn out, proven not to survive? And it of course is my great hope that the swift publication of my results will contribute to the rapid recovery of Leonardo's great painting. So I decided to turn the article into a little book.

Within days of making this decision I was able to find a publisher, thanks to the alertness and enthusiasm of my editor, Nita Tucker, who is also the editor-in-chief of the bi-weekly, *The Florentine*, surely one of the most beautiful newspapers in existence. Funding for the book's publication was immediately forthcoming thanks to the admirable generosity of my friend Peter Weller and of Friends of Florence and that fine organization's president, Simonetta Brandolini d'Adda.

In order to make the article more 'booklike' and accessible also to persons—especially Florentines—who are not students of art history or of the Italian Renaissance, I have revised the text with the great help of Victoria Miachika. She somehow managed to meet all of the very short deadlines in spite of greatly adverse conditions. The notes have remained largely the same; however, English translations of all Italian and Latin citations have been added.

I presented a first version of the study leading to this book at the Institute for Advanced Study at Princeton while I was a Member there in 1994. My renewed thanks to that justly renowned institution.

For their sage advice and criticism, my thanks to Molly Bourne, Jonathan Nelson, Brenda Preyer, Gary Radke, the late Richard Trexler and Louis Waldman. My special thanks to Maurizio Seracini for his help and encouragement.

In this book the scene that Leonardo actually began and nearly finished, representing the *Capture of a Standard*, will be termed a 'scene' or occasionally 'painting', whereas the enormous painting that Leonardo planned to make, representing the *Battle of Anghiari* and of which the *Capture of a Standard* was only a small part, will usually be called his 'battle mural' or 'mural'. Likewise the piece of cartoon by Michelangelo showing *Bathing Soldiers Reacting to a False Alarm* will be termed a 'scene', whereas the representation of the entire battle or war (probably the Battle of Cascina) that Michelangelo planned to paint will always be called his 'battle mural' or 'mural'.

There is no bibliography. Readers wishing full citations are directed to the Index, where references to all complete citations in the notes are indicated in bold under the authors' last names or the names of the archival classifications. Explanations of possibly unfamiliar Italian terms, such as *Signoria*, *intonaco* or *predella*, will also be found in the notes.

# THE CASE FOR RECOVERING THE BATTLE OF ANGHIARI

In the recently published (1993) *Ricordi* or 'Memoirs' of the noted early-sixteenth-century historian and chronicler Bartolomeo Cerretani we read:

> At this time Leonardo da Vinci, a very great and Florentine master of painting, began to paint the Hall of the Council on that wall over where the Twelve Good Men are; and that hallway from the Palace to the Hall was caused to be paved with nearly round bricks; and nine flags taken from Lord Bartolomeo d'Alviano a few days ago were hung in the said Hall.[1]

The time about which Cerretani is speaking is the summer of 1505. The hall is the enormous new trapezoidal room used by the recently constituted Major or General Council of the Florentine Republic. Then usually referred to simply as the 'Great Hall' or 'New Hall', the room today, greatly altered, is called the Salone dei Cinquecento (Hall of the Five Hundred; Fig. 1). Originally located behind it, the Hall has since been incorporated into the building we today call Palazzo Vecchio (the Old Palace), which in Leonardo's time was known as the Palazzo de' Signori (Palace of the Lords).

The Major Council, which was considered by most Florentines to be the heart of their remarkably democratic Republic, comprised all Florentine men then eligible to vote and hold office. It assembled at least once a week to decide on legislation proposed by the executive branch of the Florentine government, the *Signori e Collegi* (Lords and Colleges or Colleagues), as well as to nominate candidates for the Republic's most important offices. The councilmen present could number up to 1700.[2]

The Twelve Good Men were one of the two 'Colleges' or groups of Colleagues that assisted the *Signori* (or *Signoria*), the other being the Sixteen Gonfaloniers of the Companies of the People. For legislative purposes these three governing bodies acted as one and sat together in the Great Hall.[3]

The scene that Leonardo began and almost completed was to have been a small part of an enormous mural depicting one of the greatest victories ever achieved by the Florentine Republic, the Battle of Anghiari. In this battle, which was fought on 29 June 1440, an army of combined Florentine and Papal forces defeated a Milanese army led by the feared *condottiere* Niccolò Piccinino below the small town of Anghiari in the upper Tiber Valley.

The scene Leonardo almost finished painting, then sometimes called *The Horses* and to which I refer as the *Capture of a Standard*, was acclaimed by those who saw it as one of the most beautiful works of art in existence. But even before he could complete just this small part of his great project, Leonardo was called to Milan by the French governor of that city.[4]

Had he completed the entire mural, it would have been—at least in size—by far his greatest work. Across from or near it there was to have been another battle mural of comparable greatness representing a victory over Pisa and painted by Michelangelo. According to the sixteenth-century painter, architect and writer Giorgio Vasari, about or from whom we shall be hearing often, Michelangelo was to have painted this second mural in competition with Leonardo. The sculptor and writer Benvenuto Cellini would call the full-scale preparatory drawings or cartoons, also left unfinished, for these two paintings the 'school of the world'. He also would say that Michelangelo's hugely famous frescoes on the ceiling of the Sistine Chapel in the Vatican Palace in Rome are not half so beautiful as his battle cartoon was.[5] If these enormous murals had been painted—or just partly painted—and could still be seen today, they would most certainly rank amongst the world's foremost artistic attractions.

Leonardo's largely completed *Capture of a Standard*, whose appearance is known to us through several copies (e.g., those illustrated in Figs. 2 and 3), is generally believed to be lost. But for all we know it might still lie concealed under a counter wall or membrane built and decorated by Vasari in late 1570 and early 1571. If we can establish where the Twelve Good Men sat, we can thereby determine where Leonardo began his famous battle scene. Identifying its definite position will allow us to find out whether the painting or any remnants of it is still there.

Such a rediscovery would make one of the world's greatest paintings available once again to art lovers everywhere as well as to the people of Florence. It would also provide important information about the exact nature of the specially prepared and probably unique surface Leonardo devised on which to paint it, as well as the exact height of his great projected mural. Knowing the exact level at which Leonardo painted his scene would enable us further to determine what format Leonardo's great battle mural would likely have taken.

In addition, knowing the painting's exact location would give us a more precise idea of the seating arrangements of the *Signoria* of Florence and four committees that assisted it, as well as clarify the position of the altar in the Great Hall. It is the main purpose of this book first to present and outline several hypotheses regarding the position of the Twelve Good Men and other major officials in the Great Hall, and then to use this and other information to arrive at the probable location and size of Leonardo's battle scene.

Using a good deal of newly discovered evidence, I propose these conclusions:

1. The *Signori e Collegi* sat on the eastern side of the Hall, that is, before the long wall opposite the present entrance from the main staircase of Palazzo Vecchio (Figs. 1, 4, and 5).

2. The Twelve Good Men probably sat at the proper left of the *Signori*, that is, somewhat to our right (or towards the south) as we face the centre of the east wall.

3. The section of benches or stalls on which the Twelve sat probably began around nine Florentine *braccia*, or 5.3 metres, from the centre of the seat of the Gonfalonier of Justice,[6] who sat in the middle of the *Signoria*. We shall term this position the historic centre of the east wall.

4. The Twelve probably sat on two rows of benches and therefore occupied a space of around six *braccia*, or 3.5 metres.

5. The part of the mural that Leonardo began, representing the *Capture of a Standard and Other Military Actions,* probably measured almost three metres high by somewhat less than five metres wide.

6. The scene probably was located fairly high but not at the top of the wall, which was either 19 or, more likely, 20 *braccia* (11.1 or 11.7 metres) in height.[7]

Should any of the foregoing conclusions prove incorrect—indeed even if all of them are incorrect—we still, thanks to Cerretani, now know where Leonardo began his famous scene: 'on the wall over where the Twelve Good Men sat'. This place could not have been before either of the end walls,[8] nor could it have been either in the exact centre or far from the centre of whichever long wall it was that the *Signori e Collegi* sat before.

The new information I am presenting here suggests three interesting implications:

1. If Leonardo's famous scene or remnants of it still remains, it may now be relatively easy to locate; however, retrieving it may prove to be much more difficult.
2. Leonardo may have chosen this scene because in August of 1505 the Florentine forces had just captured several flags at a battle they won near the tower of the little coastal town of San Vincenzo. If this is the case, it is possible that the *Capture of a Standard* scene was preceded by the beginnings of another scene by Leonardo on the same wall. If it in fact exists, this other scene too might be retrievable.
3. Had Leonardo's battle mural been completed, it would have been extremely long, possibly running the entire length of the east wall. This means that Michelangelo's mural, which was to have complemented Leonardo's, was probably to have been on the opposite or west wall and may also have been planned to be extremely long.

# THE PLACE WHERE LEONARDO BEGAN: SIX CONCLUSIONS

## 1 | ON WHICH LONG WALL LEONARDO BEGAN

In his well-known *Lives of the Most Excellent Painters, Sculptors and Architects*, Giorgio Vasari states that the *Signori* or Lords of Florence were seated on the east side of the Great Hall.[9] This belief remained unchallenged until 1982, when H. Travers Newton and John Spencer contended that the *Signori* (*e Collegi*) instead sat before the middle of the somewhat shorter west wall.[10] Nicolai Rubinstein reaffirms this opinion in his excellent book on Palazzo Vecchio of 1995.[11] Unfortunately Newton and Spencer's ideas are based on some incorrect notions about where Leonardo laid the specially prepared surface on which he would paint his mural, and there are a couple of rare lapses in Rubinstein's reasoning.[12]

How can Vasari have been mistaken? He spent the better part of 12 years rebuilding and redecorating the Hall to serve as a kind of throne room for the all-powerful Duke Cosimo I de' Medici during the 1560s and early 1570s. He presumably knew it better than any other historian ever has or will. Undoubtedly in 1560, when Vasari became seriously interested in the room, it no longer looked exactly the same as it had in 1505–06, when Leonardo had painted in it. In 1512 the so-called Soderini Republic had fallen to Spanish troops sent to restore the Medici to power, and in 1530 the Last Florentine Republic had fallen to Imperial forces that likewise had been sent to reinstate that powerful family. But surely, despite the changes that the room had incurred after these political upheavals, some traces remained of where the 'magnificent and exalted' *Signori* had once sat or where the altar, which had faced the *Signori* from the opposite side of the room, had been.

The *residenza* (tribune or dais) of the *Signoria* had been made of wood and is unlikely to have survived to the time of Vasari. It had been flanked, though, by two *porticciuole* or 'little doors', both of which had lintels and doorsills of red marble.[13] During certain periods of its history the *residenza* had also been surmounted by two windows. These features were something about which Vasari evidently knew.[14] And even if no traces remained in his day of where the *residenza* had once rested or where the frame for the huge altarpiece had been, Vasari would still have been able to see traces of the doors and windows, as well as easily obtain information about the *residenza* and the altar from persons who had known them well.

Towards the end of 1512, about three months after the fall of the Soderini Republic, most or all of the Great Hall's woodwork was removed when the room was converted into a barracks to house the soldiers who now controlled the city on behalf of the Medici.[15] Much of this woodwork, including the *residenza* and the great frame for the altarpiece, which was already finished by June of 1502 even though the altarpiece itself was not begun until 1510, had been made by Baccio d'Agnolo.[16] As Baccio was also the architect in charge of the Hall during the whole Soderini Republic (1502–12) and well beyond, he evidently supervised the woodwork's removal as well.[17]

Baccio was still in charge during the Last Republic (1527–30)[18] and therefore also oversaw the restoration of the Hall that was carried out at that time. This restoration was accomplished at considerable expense,[19] no doubt in compliance with the orders given by a *Balìa* on 20 May 1527 requiring that the room be brought back to its former appearance.[20] The *Balìa* in question was a special commission that governed the Republic for several days after the second expulsion of the Medici until the Major Council was ready to resume its normal functions.

It is highly probable, then, that much of the woodwork taken out in 1512 was simply put back again in the months after May 1527.[21] Woodwork that could no longer be reinstalled at that time was likely replaced with similar woodwork crafted by the same *Capomaestro* (chief architect, foreman) of the Palace—that is, the same highly skilled furniture maker and architect, Baccio d'Agnolo—who had removed the original woodwork and even made much of it to begin with.

Vasari probably saw this replaced or restored woodwork during the four months or more (up to the autumn of 1529) he was in Florence during the Last Republic.[22] It thus is probable that the Hall that Vasari likely saw in the late 1520s was not very different from the way it had been when Leonardo had worked in it in 1505–06.[23] And Vasari, we recall, says that the *Signori* (*e Collegi*) sat on its eastern side.

In any case Vasari's authority is not necessary to prove that the *Signori e Collegi* sat before the east wall. As previously mentioned, the *residenza* or tribune of the *Signoria* was flanked by two *porticciuole* or relatively small doors. These doors separated the *Signori* from the Sixteen Gonfaloniers of the Companies on the one side and the Twelve Good Men on the other. The friezes over them were marked with golden inscriptions identifying the spaces to which the two doors provided access. One inscription read 'AUDIENTIA' and the other 'SEGRETO'.[24]

Of primary interest to us is the *Segreto*, as the *Audientia* (*Udienza*, or audience chamber) was sometimes considered just a part of the same space.[25] The *Segreto* of the Great Hall was one of at least four such spaces in the Palace.[26] In it a committee of up to 12 election officials, including two of the *Signori*, two of the Sixteen, and two of the Twelve, recorded nominations, drew names from the electoral purses (most elections were by lot) and counted votes while the Major or General Council was in session.[27]

The *Segreto* of the Great Hall was quite large. It took at least five *traina* (about 2.0 cubic metres) of wood to make its ceiling, it had at least two windows and about 14 metres of green cloth were used to cover its main desk or table (*desco*).[28] In 1512 a piece of blue cloth measuring 5.1 x 2.2 metres was bought for the *Segreto*.[29] The *Udienza* that evidently was connected to it had a fireplace, a ceiling resting on seven large beams, at least two windows and its own hallway.[30] A storage space ('maghazino') built either in or next to the *Segreto* around the time that Leonardo began painting,[31] had two floors with a combined area of perhaps 48 or 72 square metres, a staircase with 21 steps and a window probably measuring about 3.4 square metres.[32]

On 21 May 1496 a stonecutter who had been working on a window in the Great Hall was severely injured when he fell onto the 'pavement of the [Corte della] Dogana.[33] Much of the Hall had been built on top of the Dogana or Customs House, with one of its long walls facing west towards the rear of the Palace. The Hall was separated in part from the Palace by the courtyard usually known as the Corte (or Cortile) della Dogana, which corresponded more or less with its middle third. The stonecutter, then, had been working on one of the additional windows then being constructed in the middle part of the side of the Hall facing the Palace—that is, its western side.[34] As he fell all the way to the ground, it is obvious that at this time no other structures were attached to the outside of the west wall underneath this window.

If, however, the stonecutter had fallen from any of the documented windows on the government's side of the room, all of which were over the *residenza* or tribune of the *Signori* or 'over the head' of the *Collegi*, he would have fallen onto the roof of either the *Segreto* or the *Udienza* (if we may assume that these spaces already existed).[35] But the *Segreto* and *Udienza* could hardly have been attached to the outside of the middle part of the west wall—that is, the part of it that overlooked the courtyard—as there was nothing underneath to support such structures. This part of the wall rested on specially constructed piers, and it therefore would have required extremely awkward solutions to provide such support.

Moreover, it is almost unheard of for any major Italian courtyard or cloister to have one or more structures other than staircases protruding into its open space. As far as we know, nothing was ever attached to the outside of the middle part of the west wall of the Hall until the architect Battista del Tasso built the long external stairway that preceded by about two decades the grand staircase by Vasari that is there today.[36] In short there never were any *Segreto*, *Udienza* or *magazzino* on the west side of the Hall; hence the *Signori e Collegi* never sat there either.[37]

In addition, the four west wall windows appear to have been placed at a level of only three *braccia* or 1.75 metres (they are now at 1.7 metres).[38] It is highly improbable that at least two of these windows were once over the *residenza* of the *Signoria*, as it must have been at least eight *braccia* or 4.7m high.[39] Also the roofs over the *Segreto*, *Udienza* and *magazzino* must have come to a height of at least 3.5m where they met the outer wall of the Hall again making it most unlikely that these structures could have been on the Hall's western side if we consider the height at which the windows there were placed. Therefore, the *Signori e Collegi*—and with them Leonardo's scene of the *Capture of a Standard*—must have been on the eastern side of the Great Hall (Figs. 1, 4, and 5). That is the only place where other structures could have been attached, as other structures are today, to the middle of the wall on the outside. The windows in the east wall must therefore have been at a level of no less than eight *braccia* or 4.7m until they were walled up around the end of 1504.[40]

# 2 | ON WHICH SIDE OF THE WALL HE BEGAN

Of the two 'venerable Colleges' or groups of 'venerable Colleagues', that of the Twelve Good Men was the less 'honourable'. This College or group of Colleagues was created only in 1321—fifteen years after the more prestigious Sixteen Gonfaloniers of the Companies.[41] Of the two committees only the Sixteen carried flags and pennants (or had these carried for them by *pennonieri*) and were escorted home by 41 trumpeters after having been sworn into office in front of the Palace.[42] Whenever the *Collegi* are listed or mentioned separately, it is the Sixteen who are always named first. In processions it was always the Sixteen who went next to the *Signoria*.[43]

There are no useful known descriptions of how the *Signori e Collegi* were seated either in the Great Hall or elsewhere.[44] It nevertheless seems highly probable that in the Hall the Sixteen, being the more 'honourable' officials, were seated on the proper right-hand side of the *Signori*, just as Jesus 'sitteth at the right hand of the Father' and the most honoured guest sits at the host's right at a formal dinner.[45] The Twelve, therefore, must have been seated at the proper left of the *Signoria*, that is, somewhat to the right of centre (or towards the south) as one faces the east wall today (Figs. 4 and 5).

This conclusion is further supported by a simple artistic consideration. Leonardo's scene of four men fighting or trying to escape on horseback and three other men fighting or defending themselves on the ground, was—and perhaps still is—lit from the right, which is unusual for paintings of the period. This fact suggests that the seeming 'actual' source of the light seen in the painting lay to its right. In other words the dominant real light source in that part of the Hall may well have coincided more or less with the imaginary source that once appeared—and perhaps still appears—to illuminate the forms in Leonardo's scene. Such identifications of fictive light sources with real ones are familiar features in Renaissance mural paintings in which great naturalism is sought.

There probably were no windows in the east wall when Leonardo began to paint, even though at least two additional ones had been put in, evidently in 1496, over the *residenza* or tribune of the *Signoria* or 'over the head' of the *Collegi*. For these windows, as we learn from a newly found document, had been walled up around the end of 1504.[46] They were doubtless eliminated so that Leonardo and possibly also Michelangelo could paint there.

The only light sources for the east wall that a person looking at Leonardo's scene might have noticed, then, would have been the two groups of windows in the end walls. These, according to Vasari, originally had been the Hall's only source of illumination. The windows in the south wall, which is at one's right as one looks at the east wall, may all have been larger than any others in the Hall. In any case one of them—no doubt the one in the middle—almost certainly was by far the largest in the room.[47] These south windows also probably admitted the strongest light. When he designed it, then, the reason why Leonardo chose to illuminate his scene from the right was probably that he knew he was going to position the scene in the right half of the wall, closer to these south windows. That way it would look as if the light from these windows were illuminating it.

Another confirmation is found in a payment made at the beginning of 1504 to a woodworker for '28½ *braccia* (16.65m) of benches made for the passageway of the Great Hall of the Council across from the (Sixteen) Gonfaloniers'. The passageway or aisle (*andito*) in question was evidently one of two that were ordered to be completed in January of 1498 leading from the original main door of the Hall—that is, the door from the Palace—to the altar and to the *residenza* of the *Signoria* respectively (Fig. 5).[48] This entrance was at the end of the then partly open hallway connecting the new Hall with the old one on the north side of the Palace and was—and still is—in the Hall's northwest corner. The passageway in question, as well as the Sixteen Gonfaloniers, must thus have been to the north of the *residenza* of the *Signoria* or to the left of a person looking at it (if it is safe to assume that the *residenza* was on the east side of the Hall). The Twelve Good Men—and with them Leonardo's *Capture of a Standard*—would therefore have been to the south of the *residenza* or to the right of a person looking at it (Figs. 4 and 5).[49]

# 3 | THE DISTANCE OF THE SEATING AREA OF THE TWELVE FROM THE CENTRE OF THE WALL

In a record establishing the amount due to Baccio d'Agnolo for his work on the *residenza* or tribune of the *Signoria*, we read that he made 12 *braccia* of extremely costly 'cornice, frieze and architrave' for it.[50] Twelve Florentine *braccia* amounted to almost exactly seven metres. If, as seems probable, this entablature of cornice, frieze and architrave ran straight across it, the *residenza* was 12 *braccia* wide.

But it also is possible that the entablature decorated three sides of an overhang or canopy projecting up to two *braccia*, or 1.2m, from the wall behind it and that the *residenza* therefore was less wide. In any case the *residenza* cannot have been any narrower than eight *braccia*, or 4.7m, as that width would have allowed just 52cm for each of the *Signori* (if we assume that they sat in a single row).

Between the *Signori* and the Twelve was the *porticciuola* or 'little door' leading to either the *Udienza* or more likely the *Segreto* (Figs. 4 and 5). As its frieze and cornice were of marble, this 'little door' clearly was built into the wall and was not part of a wooden partition or of any other structure made of wood. The space it occupied, together with a sliver of wall on either side of it, might have been around three *braccia*, or 1.75m, but it could have been as much as two *braccia* (1.2m) more or half a *braccio* (0.3m) less. In any case the gap between the *Signoria* and the Twelve Good Men cannot have been very large. For what was evidently the same window is described once as having been over the *residenza* of the *Signoria* and once as having been 'over the head' of the Twelve.[51]

The area occupied by the Twelve thus perhaps began around nine *braccia* or 5.3m (half the probable width of the *residenza* plus the space taken up by the 'little door' and the sliver of wall on either side of it) from the wall's historic centre, that is, the centre of the throne or seat on which the Gonfalonier of Justice sat. But the distance could have been as few as six and a half *braccia* or 3.8m, or as many as eleven *braccia* or 6.4m.

As we do not yet know the exact positions of either of the two 'little doors' or one of the probably two windows over the *residenza* of the *Signori* or 'the head of' the *Collegi*,[52] we cannot say exactly where the east wall's historic centre was. This might have been determined by the middle of either the west wall or the east one and probably was aligned with the great round panel or *tondo* in the middle of the original ceiling, which no longer exists.[53] But surely this historic centre was no more than two metres from the decorative centre of the east wall as we know it today. And so, at some point probably no less than 1.8 and no more than 8.4m from the present decorative centre of the east wall, there began the part of that wall once occupied by the Twelve Good Men—and thus the area where Leonardo began to paint (Fig. 4).[54]

# 4 | THE WIDTH OF THE SEATING AREA OF THE TWELVE

According to Vasari the Republic's magistrates sat in or on a wooden *ringhiera* (gallery or platform) three *braccia* deep and three *braccia* high (1.75 x 1.75m), having seats *a uso di teatro* (of the kind used in theatres) and running all around the room. (The ordinary councilmen sat on benches on the main floor.) We also know that the access stairs and at least some of the parapet of this *ringhiera* were made of stone.[55] Given the reported depth of 1.75m and Vasari's use of the phrase, 'a uso di teatro', both Johannes Wilde and Rubinstein conclude that the *ringhiera* must have had two rows of seats.[56]

The *ringhiera* installed after the Republic's revival in May 1527 and which remained in place until October 1530, was likely seen by Vasari.[57] It may not have been the original; but even if it was not, it probably resembled the original quite closely.[58] It is not possible to verify Vasari's description by means of any itemized records that have survived.[59] We can only assume his account is correct and that there were two rows of benches or individual seats—more likely benches—on the *ringhiera*.[60]

Three other considerations make it appear that there in fact were two rows of benches or seats. One concerns the *Collegi*: if there was only one row of magistrates, the most distant members of the 'Colleges' sat far indeed (up to perhaps 13.0m) from the *Signoria*.[61] The second concerns the incredibly numerous other magistrates, of whom there may have been more than 500[62]: it is highly unlikely they could all have been accommodated in a single row. The third consideration concerns the great likelihood that the Hall of the Florentine Major Council was inspired by its Venetian counterpart.[63] The Hall of the Major Council in the Ducal Palace in Venice had two rows of seats running around it. One therefore imagines that there likewise were two rows of benches or individual seats surrounding the Great Hall of Florence (Figs. 4 and 5).

Each of the Florentine *Signori* apparently occupied around 78cm (701cm ÷ 9) of seating space. But as the *Signori* probably sat in stalls, whereas the *Collegi* evidently used benches, the members of the Colleges probably required less space.[64] A reasonable assumption is that each of them took up about one *braccio* or 58.4cm. Therefore, within the space of perhaps 3.2–3.8m (that is, six *braccia* plus or minus half a *braccio*) occupied by the Twelve Good Men, probably beginning no less than 3.8 and ending no more than 10.2m from the wall's historic centre (or no less than 1.8 or more than 12.2m from its present decorative centre), Leonardo began to paint (Figs. 4 and 5).[65]

As two of the copies (Figs. 2 and 3) reveal that one of the figures at the right of his scene, and also the standard, which likewise was to have been seen at the scene's right, remained unpainted, we may conclude that Leonardo probably worked from left to right. It is therefore likely that part of his scene lay—and perhaps still lies—to the right or south of the area once occupied by the Twelve and thus possibly was or is more than 10.2m to the right or south of the east wall's historic centre.[66]

# 5 | THE SIZE OF LEONARDO'S SCENE

Perhaps no more than 12 months after beginning to paint his battle scene, Leonardo went to Milan.[67] The *Capture of a Standard* remained partly unfinished. It probably had—and perhaps still has—an area of somewhat less than 15 square metres, as would be generally realized if the art historian Karl Frey, almost a century ago, had published the near-original of an important document instead of a paraphrase written three months later.[68]

The near-original (cited here for the first time) was written on 1 March 1513 and records a transaction made the previous 22 January, less than two months after Baccio d'Agnolo had begun to convert the Great Hall into a barracks. It reads: 'to make a protective covering ['armadura'] in the Hall of the Guard for the picture that Leonardo da Vinci made so it would not be ruined, that is: 29 boards of poplar of a third [of a *braccio*], which were 43— square *braccia* . . .'[69] Forty-three square *braccia* amounted to 14.7 square metres.

The area of the painting probably was—and perhaps still is—somewhat less, as either (1) the boards may have been fashioned into a shallow box or crate, or (2) if there was no box or crate, the boards must have been fastened directly to the wall, probably with nails, outside the painted surface. Either way the boards would have had an area somewhat greater than that of the painting.[70]

As 29 boards were used, the covering may not have been perfectly rectangular; the box or boards may simply have covered whatever painted surface there was at any given level or interval. The scene's proportions appear to have been around 5:8, so it probably was—or, if it survives, still is—almost three metres high at its highest point and somewhat less than five metres wide at its widest.

The figures in it probably were or are slightly larger than life-sized (perhaps between 2.0 and 2.3m tall if they had been or were standing). They thus would have been or be similar in size to the main figures in many of the most important monumental wall paintings of the period, such as Leonardo's own *Last Supper* in the refectory of the convent of Santa Maria delle Grazie in Milan or Raphael's *Parnassus* in the *Stanze* in the Vatican Palace in Rome.

The scene must therefore have been or be situated in either the foreground of the projected battle mural (that is, near its bottom) or its middle ground (around its lower middle). In mural painting an artist normally works from top to bottom in order not to drip paint on what he or she has already painted. It therefore is likely that Leonardo did not intend to paint any other figures or important forms above his scene of the *Capture*. It appears, then, that Leonardo's whole battle mural was not intended to be very high.

# 6 | THE DISTANCE FROM THE FLOOR OF LEONARDO'S SCENE

One of the contemporary sources reports that Leonardo's *stucco* 'high up there' (in Italian the word *stucco* normally means 'putty' rather than 'plaster' as it does in English) did not dry properly because the heat from the charcoal fires Leonardo had used to dry this oil-based surface preparation had failed to reach the upper part of the wall. Therefore the upper part of the surface ran, whereas the *stucco* 'down low' did dry properly.

To judge from the surviving copies (e.g., the paintings illustrated in Figs. 2 and 3), one of which is dated 1553,[71] there do not appear to have been any major defects in the upper part of Leonardo's scene, indicating that Leonardo did not paint on the *stucco* 'high up there' if it really failed to dry. Also, as previously mentioned, Leonardo's figures probably were slightly larger than life-sized, suggesting that his group was to have been seen relatively low in the battle mural. The *Capture of a Standard* certainly does not appear to have been intended as background material.

At what level, then, was the entire battle mural to have begun? Vasari writes that the wooden *ringhiera* or magistrates' gallery running around the Great Hall was three *braccia* (1.75m) high, and there is evidence to support this statement.[72] Behind the *ringhiera* there were wooden *spalliere* or pieces of wainscotting, which must have been at least two *braccia* high.[73] The woodwork must therefore have come to a height of at least five *braccia* or 2.9m, making it impossible for the mural to have begun any lower. In the middle of the wall was the *residenza* or tribune of the *Signoria*, which, with its surmounting 'cornice, frieze and architrave', must have been at least eight *braccia* or 4.7m high. Obviously Leonardo's battle mural could not have begun any lower than that where the *residenza* was.

In the artist's agreement or 'contract' of May 1504 with the *Signoria* of Florence, the mural is called a 'quadro' (rectangular panel, picture), leading one to suppose that it was expected to be perfectly rectangular. The mural's probably rectangular format, combined with the near-certainty that part of it had to be over the *residenza*, makes it appear likely that the bottom edge of the mural throughout its entire length was to have been at least at the level established by the top of the *residenza* or eight *braccia* (4.7m).[74]

But there may have been another feature in the wall that determined the level at which the battle mural was to have begun. The frescoes by Vasari that are now on the two long walls of the Hall (Fig. 1) are painted on 'incrustations' of terracotta or mostly of terracotta that have a probable thickness of 15.6cm.[75] One would expect these incrustations, which are supported by huge stone frames, to project from the rest of the wall by at least as much as their thickness, but instead they are perfectly flush with it.

The rest of the wall, then, must be thicker underneath the incrustations than it is where they are located, in effect creating a now invisible setback or ledge at the level at which are positioned the stone strips upon which the incrustations rest. This now invisible ledge must be at least 15.6cm deep and is situated at a level of eight *braccia* or 4.7m (Fig. 4).[76] It is possible that the ledge already existed during the time of Leonardo, at which time it still would have been visible.

Art diagnostician Maurizio Seracini, who has been searching for Leonardo's painting for more than 30 years, has observed that the masonry one could see when the plaster was removed from underneath the strips supporting the frames and incrustations in the east wall, appears to be similar to the masonry found elsewhere in the original late-fifteenth-century walls of the Hall.

Moreover, Seracini points out, the lower parts of the windows that once were in the west wall, some of which were first rediscovered when the plaster was removed from parts of the outside of this wall around 1975, are also visible from the inside by means of thermography. This fact may indicate that the thicker piece of wall in which the lower parts of these now invisible windows are found and which creates the ledge in question, is entirely original. For if Vasari, in order to make this ledge, had placed a new layer of masonry in front of a piece of wall originally having the same thickness as the rest of the wall and into which the lower parts of the former windows had afterwards been built (in 1496), his new outer layer ought now to conceal these lower parts from thermography.[77]

The now invisible ledge that supports Vasari's frames and incrustations in the west wall may therefore be part of the Hall's original construction. And if it is, the identical ledge in the east wall clearly is original also. Surely, if this ledge in the east wall already existed and was still visible when Leonardo was preparing his battle mural, he would not have planned the mural to begin any lower than the level at which it is situated, or eight *braccia* (4.7m). This eventuality would also provide a simple explanation of why Vasari's frescoes begin where they do.

If, on the other hand, it was Vasari who built the now invisible ledge by reinforcing the bottom of the wall so he could place his frames and incrustations on top of it,[78] let us hope he positioned it and the enormous frames it supports in such a way as to avoid damaging Leonardo's *Capture of a Standard*. Vasari showed such precaution when he protected Masaccio's famous fresco of the *Trinity* (or, better, *Throne of Grace*, in which the Trinity and the Crucifixion are combined) in the Florentine church of Santa Maria Novella by positioning an altarpiece with a large stone frame in front of the fresco in such a way that it did not touch it.[79]  If he did the same with the incrustation in front of Leonardo's scene, that scene began—and probably still begins—at a height of no less than 5.65m, or the level to which the bottom parts of Vasari's frames now come.  In that case the painting is probably still located somewhere behind that artist's fresco of the *Battle of Marciano* (Fig. 1, far right).[80]

The scene of the *Capture of a Standard* as we know it today is not likely to have been situated at the very bottom of Leonardo's projected battle mural.  In both of the two most reliable copies (Figs. 2 and 3), we see that two legs of one of the horses have been cut off.  Perhaps Leonardo was unable to finish the lower parts of these limbs because they came below the level of the platform from which he worked.  The completed legs would not have reached all the way to the bottom of the battle mural either, as the figures in Leonardo's larger paintings are always placed somewhat back in space, that is, somewhat above the bottom edge of the painting.

The greatest likelihood therefore is that Leonardo's scene began—and perhaps still begins—somewhere around the middle or upper middle of the wall.  The wall's paintable surface possibly came to the height of the duke's *Udienza* by Baccio Bandinelli and others at the north end of the Hall (Fig. 1, middle), or 18 *braccia* (10.5m).  In any case it went no higher than to a level of 19 *braccia* or 11.1m (Fig. 4).[81]  The scene is unlikely to have begun or begin any higher than at 7.3m, as there probably was not enough room for it—plus a small amount of background or sky—beyond that level.

If Leonardo's *Capture* survives and can be relocated, knowing the exact level at which it is painted should enable us to determine what format Leonardo intended his great battle mural to have. If, as seems probable, the scene begins fairly high on the wall (at a level of around six or six and a half metres), then the mural was not planned to be very tall but would, because of its great size (to be discussed presently), have had to be very long indeed. If, on the other hand, the scene begins relatively low (at around four or four and a half metres), then it is probable that the mural was planned to be quite tall, as it no doubt was to have reached all the way to the cornice under the ceiling. In that case it might not have been planned to be very long.

To sum up: Leonardo probably began his great mural with a largely completed scene measuring almost three metres high by somewhat less than five metres wide and at least partly located between around 3.8 and 10.2m to the right of the historic centre of the east wall of the Great Hall. The bottom of this painting possibly rested at a level of no less than 5.3 and no more than 7.3m.[82] The bottom edge of the finished scene—as well as the entire battle mural—possibly would have been at no less than 4.7 and no more than 6.7m.

# THREE POSSIBLE IMPLICATIONS

## 1 | FINDING LEONARDO'S SCENE

**If Leonardo's famous scene or remnants of it still remains, it may now be relatively easy to locate; however, retrieving it may prove to be much more difficult.**

The most important implication of the previous discussion should be obvious: Leonardo's *Capture of a Standard*—or at least remnants of it—might still exist, and the preceding arguments establish its most likely location. As the scene was to have been part of Leonardo's most ambitious painting and was acclaimed as one of the greatest artistic achievements of an age that boasts such triumphs as Leonardo's own *Last Supper* and *Mona Lisa*, Michelangelo's *David* and Sistine Ceiling, Raphael's *School of Athens* and Titian's *Assunta*,[83] it surely warrants a renewed search. Locating the painting—if it still exists—should no longer be unduly difficult, but freeing it may prove to be an extremely complicated task.

When Vasari rebuilt and redecorated the Hall, he raised its ceiling by probably 12 *braccia* or 7.0m (Fig. 1).[84] He resurfaced the parts of the two long walls on which he painted his own battle frescoes with six 'incrustations' (*incrostature*) of *mezzane rozze campigiane* (or *alla campigiana*).[85]

*Mezzane* are thin, wide pieces of terracotta traditionally measuring one half by one quarter of a *braccio* (in and around Florence 29.2 x 14.6cm). Today they are used mostly for flooring or roofing. The *campigiana* type, which was thicker and more expensive than the ordinary one, is now no longer made. *Mezzane campigiane* were usually around 3cm thick and normally used, the way bricks are today, to build walls, arches, and other structures.

Applied vertically, like tiles, with their broad faces showing, 21 of these *mezzane* were more than enough to cover a square metre of wall, and 9,870 of them would have sufficed to incrust the area occupied by Vasari's frescoes (around 470m²). However, at least 39,243 were supplied. That was almost four times the number needed to incrust this area if the *mezzane* were applied vertically.[86]

If, on the other hand, the *mezzane* were laid flat and across in a single course, with their long sides showing, up to 83 of them were needed to build a square metre of counter wall. The thickness of such a wall after plastering would have been about 15.6cm (the width of a *mezzana* plus about 1cm of plaster).[87] In that case the number of *mezzane* needed was about 39,010, a number that corresponds very closely to the 39,243 recorded to have been supplied.[88]

It therefore seems apparent that Vasari's 'incrustations' are pieces of counter wall or membranes about 15.6cm thick, at least in most places.[89]

Moreover, in 2002 a penetrating radar scan performed on the incrustations encountered interferences at a depth of about 15cm, indicating the presence of some kind of interface at that depth. The incrustation at the southern end of the east wall, which was the last to be built and is probably the one that interests us most, exhibited particularly pronounced interferences, indicating the likely presence there of a large air gap—that is, a space between the incrustation and the original wall.[90]

Vasari's incrustations are 7.5m high; and, as we have just seen, the counter wall, evidently made mostly of terracotta,[91] clearly appears to be only around 15.6cm thick. Unfortunately such a thin counter wall would need, for purposes of stability, to be joined or tied in numerous places to the main wall behind it. Such joinings would have disastrous consequences for any painting on that wall unless the joins or ties have been positioned in such a way as to minimize damage to it.

Why did Vasari make these 'incrustations'? The plaster surfaces of Renaissance walls are often uneven and often suffer from cracking, peeling, leakage, humidity and other defects. Chances are that the surfaces of the original walls of the Great Hall, which were built in extreme haste, exhibited at least some of these flaws. The surfaces on which Vasari painted his frescoes, by contrast, are, with one exception, remarkably flat, smooth and dry. The primary purpose of Vasari's incrustations almost certainly was to create new surfaces on which to paint that would be largely independent of the original walls and thus free of their defects.[92] Vasari no doubt found it easier to make new surfaces of his own than to work with the ones already there. He also must have wanted to reinforce the original walls, which he was raising by no less than 7.0m.

In 1980 about 10 square metres of Vasari's fresco of the *Rout of San Vincenzo* were detached and a few of the *mezzane* removed from the incrustation in the south side of the west wall during an unsuccessful attempt to relocate Leonardo's painting. This search is documented by a series of photographs including a few showing the *mez-*

*zane* as well as an *intonaco* surface beneath them evidently belonging to the original wall.[93]  From these photographs and the previously mentioned penetrating radar scan, Maurizio Seracini concludes that the incrustations do not touch the original walls in places and are probably joined to them by means of stone or metal ties.

Considering their remarkable straightness and apparent uniformity (they appear consistently to have the thickness of the width of one *mezzana* plus a small amount of plaster), it indeed seems probable that these almost perfectly flat structures do not always make contact with the no doubt uneven original surfaces beneath them.  There is, to be sure, the unlikely and unwelcome chance that the incrustations have been cemented to the original wall.  Seracini, however, believes this chance to be negligible particularly in the case of the right-hand or southern panel of the east wall, where the penetrating radar scan encountered especially pronounced interferences at a depth of about 15cm indicating the probable presence of an air gap there.  This incrustation, on which is painted Vasari's *Battle of Marciano*, was the last to be built and is likely the one that concerns us most.[94]

If Vasari in fact deliberately left a large space between the incrustation and the original wall here, he may have done so in order to make this part of the east wall straighter and more closely parallel to the west wall than it had been previously.  Or perhaps he did so in order to avoid having to destroy Leonardo's painting.

Leonardo's *Capture of a Standard* is not the only important Florentine mural painting to have been covered up by Vasari.  When he was directing the redecoration of the church of Santa Maria Novella, Vasari saw to it that an altarpiece with a large stone frame he was having installed in front of Masaccio's famous *Trinity* fresco was positioned so that it did not touch it.[95]  Vasari no doubt expected this installation to be permanent and did not suppose that Masaccio's *Trinity* would ever be seen again. Yet today we enjoy this marvelous painting, and whatever damages it has suffered were, for the most part, not inflicted by or because of Vasari. It thus is quite possible that Vasari's incrustation on the right-hand or south side of the east wall in the Great Hall does not even touch the surface on which Leonardo appears to have painted. If so, we should soon be able to admire his famous scene.

These conclusions are at once encouraging and discouraging: encouraging because if Leonardo's painting still exists, it appears that Vasari's 'incrustation' may have been affixed to the wall in such a way as to minimize the damage to the surface on which Leonardo painted it; discouraging because it will be extremely difficult to free the painting, if it still exists, from underneath a 15.6cm-thick counter wall that is covered with a fresco by Vasari—not to mention that this counter wall must also be joined or tied in numerous places to the wall that bears the painting and possibly even to the painting itself.

If it survives, relocating Leonardo's painting should not be unduly difficult, even if it currently languishes under an 'incrustation' and is perhaps covered by whitewash or plaster. Seracini believes that it may be possible to locate by means of thermography (applied to the back of the wall from outside the room) at least one of the *porticciuole*, or 'little doors', that once flanked the *residenza* or tribune of the *Signoria* and thus determine the probable position of the historic centre of the east wall of the Great Hall (Figs. 4 and 5).

To locate just one *porticciuola*—the one to our left or to the north—ought to be sufficient. The other was around 13 or 14 *braccia* (7.6 or 8.2m) to the right or south of it and likely was at least partly situated in the space now occupied by a large doorway.[96] Seracini has found evidence of a piece of arch in the upper part of the east wall. He believes this piece of arch to have been part of one of the probably two windows that were once over the *Signori* (or else the *Collegi*). These windows existed from 1496 until shortly before Leonardo began to paint and were then filled with stones and mortar and perhaps reopened or partly reopened in or by 1513.[97]

As it is a short distance to the right or south of the wall's centre, the window to which this piece of arch once belonged—if Seracini is right—may well be the one that was 'over the head' of the Twelve Good Men. It would therefore be very close to the place where Leonardo began to paint. The rediscovery of the other window(s), or part(s) of it (them), would also help us locate the wall's historic centre.[98]

With great luck one can get even closer. If, as seems very likely, there are large spaces or air gaps between the 'incrustation' and the original wall in the area between 3.8 and 15.0m to the right of the east wall's historic centre, one naturally hopes to find one measuring almost three metres high by somewhat less than five metres across. If they exist, such air gaps can probably be detected by means of high-sensitivity ultrasonic or penetrating radar scans. Determining the positions of the stone or metal ties that likely join the incrustation to the original wall might be possible by means of such scans or high-sensitivity thermography. If such ties in fact exist and can be detected, a number of them might be found to surround or otherwise reveal the presence of the area we are seeking.

Once the scene's probable position has been established as accurately as possible, there still will be the problem of how to look behind or through the 'incrustation' to determine whether the scene still exists without disturbing Vasari's fresco any more than necessary. Undoubtedly today's diverse and sophisticated technologies will provide some satisfactory means to locate the mural—if it is still there.

Finding the scene should not be very difficult. For if it survives, our target probably has an area of at least 12 square metres. And judging from the amount of linseed oil and 'Greek' pitch that was bought to make the specially prepared surface for the painting, this surface must have (or once have had) an area of at least 20 square metres and probably a good deal more.[99]

The real difficulties will begin only if and when the painting is rediscovered. Freeing an extremely fragile as well as priceless mural painting, probably in oil and of considerable size, from underneath a counter wall or membrane bearing another important painting, will be a formidable task for even the Florentine restorers.

What emerges, if the painting is still there and can somehow be uncovered, may be disappointing. Three first-hand accounts state or imply that already in the mid-sixteenth century the painting was in poor condition, due largely to the way that Leonardo had prepared the surface on which he painted it.[100] An inspection of the copies shows that it may have been deteriorating noticeably before it was covered up or destroyed around the end of 1570.[101] If it was not destroyed at that time, the scene must nevertheless have suffered during the two times the Hall was occupied by soldiers. Further damage must have occurred when Vasari raised the wall on which it is painted, and again when he put a huge stone frame around or across the piece of wall it occupies, and yet again when he built his incrustation in front of it.

But the painting still was in good enough condition in 1549—that is, probably *after* Vasari wrote his dismissive words about it (but before he renovated the Hall)—that the writer Anton Francesco Doni, a friend of Michelangelo, could consider it in that year to be one of the most beautiful works in Florence and call it 'a miraculous thing'.[102] And the fact that two of Vasari's frescoes in the

Hall today—one of them most likely in the place where the *Capture* was or is and the other across from it—clearly appear to contain motifs borrowed from Leonardo's painting, inclines one to believe that Vasari could still see the painting before he built his incrustation in front of it.

It is entirely possible, then, that the *Capture of a Standard*, or at least some of it, still survives. For all we know, its condition might be no worse than that of Leonardo's hugely famous *Last Supper* in Milan.[103]

# 2 | WHEN AND WHY
## LEONARDO BEGAN THE SCENE

**Leonardo may have chosen the *Capture of a Standard* scene because in August of 1505 the Florentine forces had just captured several flags at a battle they won near the tower of the little coastal town of San Vincenzo. If this is the case, it is possible that this scene was preceded by the beginnings of another scene by Leonardo on the same wall. If it in fact exists, this other scene too might be retrievable.**

Until a few decades ago it was generally believed that Leonardo began to paint his *Capture of a Standard* during the early spring of 1505. His agreement with the *Signoria* of Florence, dated 4 May 1504, required him to finish the cartoon or full-scale preparatory drawing for his mural by 28 February 1505 or else start painting even if he had not yet completed it (which he probably had not).[104] Also March and April are when several payment records show him to have been active in the Hall.

But in one of his *Madrid Codices*, notebooks that were not rediscovered until the 1960s, there is an entry dated 6 June 1505 in which Leonardo writes about starting to 'color' in the Palace. In it Leonardo describes how, as he was about to 'put down' or 'lay' his brush—that is, apply it to the wall—the weather broke and the bell rang to summon 'the men' to their deliberations. He also complains that (because of the storm) his cartoon tore, the water spilled and the jug for bringing the water Leonardo and his assistants were using broke.[105]  It is possible that 6 June 1505 was the day when Leonardo started painting his great mural and that he regarded the outbreak of the storm and the ringing of the bell as not just unfortunate occurrences but bad omens.[106]  In that case his previous activity in the Hall evidently had entailed only the preparation of (and experimentation with) the special surface on which he would paint, the transfer of his design to the wall, and other preparations.[107]  In any case it is certain that Leonardo began to paint—or at least tried to—no later than 6 June 1505.[108]

Bartolomeo Cerretani, however, speaks of Leonardo's beginning to paint in connexion with two other events that took place next to or in the Great Hall: the completion of the entranceway's new flooring and the display in the Hall itself of nine (or 13) flags captured by the Florentine troops at the Rout of San Vincenzo.[109]

It is difficult to determine exactly when the new flooring was completed; we know only that 1060 hexagonal tiles were bought for it some time in May or June of 1505.[110]  Regarding the captured flags we can be more precise: the Rout of San Vincenzo occurred on 17 August of the same year, and the flags were hung in the Hall two days later.[111]

It is not easy to reconcile the information found in the *Madrid Codices* with that provided by Cerretani.  If Leonardo began to paint—or at least tried to—on or before 6 June 1505, why does Cerretani imply that he began around 19 August?  Did Leonardo begin twice?  Did the storm damage his cartoon so greatly that he lost more than two months repairing it?  Was Leonardo so discouraged by the storm that he did not try to paint again for more than two months?  Does Cerretani's statement concern a part of the mural other than the one that was—or at least was to have been—started on or before 6 June?  Is Cerretani extremely imprecise or simply confused?

What is of greater interest is why Leonardo should have started with the *Capture of a Standard* and in the place where he evidently did. In one of the most authoritative accounts of the Battle of Anghiari, we read that a successful assault on an enemy standard, involving hundreds of men and horses, was what led to the Florentine victory.[112] The assault and the capture of the standard therefore were the beginning of the end of the battle.

Before the capture there was a fight at a bridge that also seems to have interested Leonardo.[113] The entire battle mural probably was to have begun at the right or to the south with a scene of a reserve corps about to go into action from that side (Fig. 7), in keeping with what Leonardo prescribes in one of his notes.[114] In this scene too the light was to have come from the right. Therefore, it is likely that *Capture of a Standard*, in which the action quite unusually goes from right to left, was to have been at least the third in a sequence of interflowing scenes reading from right to left against a single background and possibly running across the whole east wall of the Great Hall.[115] After it there surely would have been more. The four horsemen in the scene are not only racing to capture the standard or escape with it. They are also dashing towards the next scene, whatever that was to have been.

Why did Leonardo begin near the middle of the wall? Why did he not start, as Michelangelo apparently was going to, at one side or at the beginning of the whole sequence or 'story'? (Or did he, on or before 6 June 1505?) If he did not wish to begin at the side, why did Leonardo not begin with the action in the very middle, where the windows had just been eliminated and the Gonfalonier of Justice sat? Was he prevented from doing so by the presence there of the *residenza* of the *Signoria* with its *aliette* or 'little wings', or might there have been some other reason?

Cerretani speaks of Leonardo's beginning to paint in the same sentence in which he reports the display in the Hall of the flags captured at San Vincenzo. One is therefore tempted to suppose that the *Capture of a Standard* somehow relates to the display of those flags, as well as to the victory, which, Cerretani says, was held to be the Republic's greatest 'in the last hundred years and even 200'.[116]

This is not to suggest that Leonardo invented his scene of the *Capture* because of the Rout of San Vincenzo. Everything we know about the preparations for his great mural indicates that by the time that battle took place, Leonardo had already spent a good deal of time developing this scene.[117] And well before he started to paint he must already have had a clear idea of how the scene would be positioned in relation to the other scenes that would form his great battle mural.[118] The standard to be depicted—or perhaps actually attached to the pole in the painting—was one of two captured at Anghiari. These flags were among the major trophies of the Florentine Republic and no doubt of particular interest to the Gonfalonier (Standard-Bearer) of Justice, in whose room they possibly still hung.[119] In short, the scene of the *Capture of a Standard* must already have existed in cartoon form well before the Rout of San Vincenzo occurred.

But if Leonardo in fact began to paint the *Capture* when Cerretani implies he did, that is, in August of 1505, what was it that prompted him to start painting that particular scene at that particular time? Might he have started to paint it because of the Rout of San Vincenzo and the captured flags? Might some government official have ordered or asked him to do so? Leonardo in all likelihood had already been painting for at least two months and eleven days when the Rout of San Vincenzo occurred. He would therefore have already been working on a different scene and interrupted his work on it in order to paint the *Capture* instead. If so, there once were—and possibly still are—the beginnings of another scene by Leonardo on the east wall of the Great Hall also, perhaps near that wall's southern end.[120]

It is possible that the Gonfalonier (Standard-Bearer) of Justice and the Sixteen Gonfaloniers of the Companies had their standards with or near them when they assembled in the Great Hall. Surely the nine (or 13) flags taken at San Vincenzo might be seen there—perhaps upside down—from 19 August 1505 on. Still other flags probably could be seen there as well. Is it not attractive to imagine the standard that Leonardo was to have painted in his scene of the *Capture* in the company of all these other flags? Or could it be that one or, in alternation, both of the real standards captured at Anghiari were going to be hung from the pole that Leonardo painted in his scene?

# 3 | LEONARDO AND MICHELANGELO IN THE GREAT HALL

**Had Leonardo's battle mural been completed, it would have been extremely long, possibly running the entire length of the east wall. This means that Michelangelo's mural, which was to have complemented Leonardo's, was probably to have been on the opposite or west wall and may also have been planned to be extremely long.**

According to Vasari, the Great Hall was originally designed (in 1495) with six large windows: three at either end. But, Vasari says, upon its rapid completion the planners realised that, due to its great size and low proportions, the Hall had insufficient light. And so (almost certainly in 1496) they put in another six windows: two in the middle of the east wall and four in the west wall.[121] As far as we can determine, this information is accurate.[122] Vasari also reports that the citizens intended in time to decorate the Hall with paintings.[123] Here too he surely is correct. If two external walls well over 50 metres long were first designed without windows, it is probable indeed that they were designed that way so that mural paintings or other decorations could be applied to them.

After it had been ordered by public decree that Leonardo should be awarded some beautiful work to paint in the Great Hall, Vasari somewhat fancifully writes, the artist was commissioned to paint the Hall (*gli fu allogata la detta Sala*) by the Gonfalonier of Justice, Piero Soderini. (In fact he was commissioned by the whole *Signoria* to paint a 'quadro' [rectangular panel, picture] or a 'pictura'.) Later on Soderini, seeing the great *virtù* (ability) of Michelangelo, commissioned that artist to paint 'a part of that Hall', so that he might do 'the other wall' (*l'altra facciata*) in competition with Leonardo.[124] (We do not know who really commissioned Michelangelo. It certainly was not Soderini and does not appear to have been the *Signoria* either. It therefore might have been the *Operai* of the Palace.) Vasari also states that Michelangelo's cartoon for his projected battle mural was 'grandissimo'.

Michelangelo himself says in a letter: 'I had undertaken to do half of the Hall of the Council of Florence, that is, to paint it, for which I [was supposed to have] had three thousand ducats'.[125] These two contemporary sources, which are the only extant sources that enable us to ascertain where Michelangelo was to have painted, suggest, along with some documentary evidence, that the two artists were to have painted something very large indeed on their respective sides of the Hall: Leonardo necessarily on the east wall and Michelangelo therefore on the west. Three thousand ducats is, according to Michelangelo himself, the amount he received for his work on the ceiling of the Sistine Chapel in the Vatican Palace in Rome. The Sistine Ceiling, along with the lunettes or round wall segments over the windows that Michelangelo also painted, has an area of well over $750m^2$.

But in 1944 Johannes Wilde challenged the belief that the two great murals were to have been painted on opposite walls in his fundamental study on the Hall, in which he proposes a reconstruction that has generally been accepted to this day.[126] Taking as his point of departure a window that is still mostly visible on the outside of the Hall's north wall and has an *occhio* (oculus, or round window) above it, Wilde envisions a room in which all the windows were the same size, all had *occhi* of the same size above them and all were positioned at the same level. Wilde imagines the four windows on the west wall of which Vasari speaks to have been spaced almost evenly. Assuming that all of the windows were positioned at the same level, he pictures the probably two on the east wall to have flanked the *residenza* or tribune of the *Signoria* rather than been over it; they thus would have been at least 11 metres apart. (Wilde of course did not know that these windows had been eliminated shortly before Leonardo began to paint.)

Wilde therefore reasons that there was no room for a huge painting on the west wall and concludes that the murals of Leonardo and Michelangelo consequently were both to have gone on the east wall, in the spaces at its two sides between the corners of the room and the two windows that Wilde imagines still to have existed as well as to have flanked the *residenza* of the *Signoria*. He estimates that each of the two murals was to have measured about 12 by 30 *braccia* (7 x 17.5m) or 122.5m².[127]

In most of these respects Wilde is in error. For the windows were not all the same size,[128] did not all have *occhi* or round windows above them (and the *occhi* that did exist were not all the same size either)[129] and were not all placed at the same level.[130] The windows on the west wall, which were about 4.5m high, were almost certainly much smaller than one of the three on the south wall and possibly smaller than the other two there as well. They may not have been spaced at all evenly, they did not have *occhi* above them and they appear to have been placed at a height of only three *braccia* or 1.75m (now 1.7m)—that is, the probable level of the floor of the *ringhiera* or magistrates' gallery that ran around the Hall.[131] As already discussed, the relatively small windows on the east wall, which had been placed much higher (probably at a level of at least eight *braccia* or 4.7m), no longer existed when Leonardo began to paint. They had been walled up towards the end of 1504, no doubt so that he and—in the unlikely event that Wilde is right—also Michelangelo could paint there.[132]

All of the considerations that lead Wilde to conclude that the two great murals were to have been at the sides of a single wall rather than on opposite walls, as contemporary sources seem to indicate, are based on incomplete knowledge (as Wilde acknowledges) and (clearly stated) assumptions that have since proved to be incorrect.

In fact there is no compelling reason to believe that one of the murals—necessarily the one by Michelangelo—could not have been planned for the west wall, even after that wall had been redesigned to have (probably) four windows.[133] As far as we know there were no obstructions on it from the tops of the windows and the frame for the altarpiece, both of which came to a level of around eleven *braccia* or 6.4m, to the *cornicione* or cornice beneath the ceiling, a distance of no less than seven *braccia* or 4.1m and no more than eight *braccia* or 4.7m. And from a previously uncited record we learn that Michelangelo in fact worked from a platform resting on trestles or sawhorses four *braccia* or 2.35m high while preparing the upper parts of his cartoon.[134] The cartoon, the height of which probably corresponded to the height of Michelangelo's projected battle mural,[135] therefore might, as the size of the figures would also lead one to suppose, have been around 4.1-4.6m high. This was approximately the height of the space over the windows on the west wall. This wall, one imagines, must have been redesigned the way it was, with relatively small windows placed as low as possible—that is, at the probable level of the floor of the *ringhiera*—in order to leave room for paintings above them, in keeping with what had reportedly been envisioned when the Hall was first designed.[136]

That the two great battle murals were to have gone on opposite walls, as well as too have been extremely long, was forcefully if erratically argued by Christian-Adolf Isermeyer in 1964. As Isermeyer points out, Leonardo received at least 252 square metres of paper.[137] He also received at least 88 Florentine pounds or 29.9 kilogrammes of sifted flour to make paste to assemble his cartoon, the drawing of which he probably did not complete, and perhaps 17.6 metres or more of cloth to make a hem for it.[138] This paper, paste and cloth sufficed to create a usable hemmed surface of at least 223 square metres.[139] The three *quaderni* (at least 19.9m$^2$) of paper afterwards given to Leonardo *per la pictura* ('for the picture'), which were enough to create a usable surface of at least 17.6m$^2$, most likely served to make a simplified duplicate of the *Capture of a Standard* section. Artists often made such duplicates so they would not ruin the often beautifully drawn master cartoons while transferring the designs on them to the surfaces to be painted.[140]

It is not necessary to assume that the amount of master cartoon on which Leonardo drew, or intended to draw, before starting to paint was the full 223m$^2$ or more for which paper was available. For even if we do not, we still must conclude that the area for which he prepared, or intended to prepare, was a great deal more than the 122.5m$^2$ for which Wilde allows. And whatever it was, this area may not have corresponded to all of Leonardo's battle mural anyway.[141]

It is difficult to imagine two battle murals of such scale on a single wall of the Great Hall. Except where the *residenza* was, they would have had to be even taller than the 7m height estimated by Wilde,[142] and battle paintings of such height did not, as far as we know, exist at the time. It also is difficult to believe that the cartoons were or were to have been over 7m high in most places. How could they have been transported and utilized if they were that tall?

And could the rooms in which they were prepared have accommodated cartoons of such height?

In any case we have strong evidence that Michelangelo's cartoon was no more than 4.6m high.[143] While we have reason to believe that the height of Michelangelo's cartoon corresponded to the height of his projected battle mural, we unfortunately do not know whether this was the case with Leonardo's cartoon also. If both murals were intended for a single wall, they obviously would have had to be designed to be the same height and probably also the same size, but it is far from certain that they in fact were so designed.[144] If conversely they were to have been different in height—as our evidence suggests they were—then clearly they were intended for different walls.

Finally, it is difficult to imagine enormous murals by Leonardo and Michelangelo coexisting on a single wall of the Great Hall. How would these two murals have related to each other? Michelangelo's would undoubtedly have been in fresco, with bright but relatively pale 'earth' colours, and possibly consisting of separately framed scenes; whereas Leonardo's would probably have been in oil, with relatively dark and rich 'furnace' colours, and probably consisting of one continuous space.[145] How could two such fundamentally different paintings have met successfully in the middle of the wall? Were they simply to have collided there, creating a sense of imbalance in the room as a whole and leaving a weak thin line of framing elements over the Gonfalonier of Justice and the planned statue of the *Holy Saviour* that would have split the room visually?[146] In that case both murals would have had to increase in height once they had cleared the *residenza* or tribune of the *Signoria*.

Or was there instead, as Wilde believes, to have been a sizeable gap between the two murals, possibly filled with captured flags, other trophies, and even a clock, as well as the *residenza*?[147] But if the latter, why had it been decided to eliminate the windows over the *residenza*, and how could two murals each approaching at least 223m² in area possibly have fit?

The strong likelihood, then, is that the two murals were to have been on opposite walls. Leonardo evidently was to have produced a mural extending across all or most of the east wall. He was supposed to have made 'a great work', the Gonfalonier of Justice wrote to the French governor of Milan. This work would have been as awesome (and was as unrealiseable) in its scale as the great bronze horse Leonardo was unable to complete for his projected monument to Duke Francesco Sforza in Milan. But, in the Gonfalonier's words, Leonardo had made only 'a small beginning' on his great mural, even though the Republic had already paid him a good sum of money for it. (In the opinion of the *Signoria*, Leonardo had not even started!)[148]

Michelangelo therefore was evidently to have painted his mural on the west wall. According to the same Gonfalonier, this mural would have been 'an amazing thing'.[149] Michelangelo's piece of cartoon, which is now known only through a copy painted by Aristotile da Sangallo, showed an episode preceding the battle Michelangelo apparently was to have depicted (Fig. 6). This fact, along with a few others to be discussed shortly, suggests that the piece of cartoon corresponded to just the beginning of Michelangelo's mural and that much more was to have followed.[150] The scene evidently was an introduction or prelude—the first scene in a sequence—and therefore intended for the left or southern part of this wall. The forms in it were to have been illuminated from the left and would therefore probably have appeared to be lit by the same south windows, one of which was the largest in the room, that also seemed to illuminate Leonardo's *Capture of a Standard*.[151]

Michelangelo's battle mural thus probably was to have been seen over the Great Hall's altar or 'chapel', which was dedicated to the Virgin Mary. This altar's great unfinished *Altarpiece of the Major Council*, by Fra Bartolomeo (begun only in 1510; Fig. 8), contains, according to Vasari, all the protector-saints of Florence and those saints on whose feast days the Republic had been victorious in battle.[152] The idea would have been that Mary, who naturally is the central figure in the painting, not only watched over the city but also helped it in battle. Mary was believed to have saved Florence on several occasions from both natural disasters and military threats, and she would be expected to help the Florentine armies defeat the Imperial forces during the Siege of Florence of 1529–30 (which unfortunately they did not), just as Jesus was thought to have delivered Florence from the tyranny of Piero de' Medici and would be expected to favor its armies during the Siege of Florence also, and just as the Major Council was claimed to have been ordained by God.[153] One might almost think of the Mary in Fra Bartolomeo's altarpiece as another 'Madonna della Battaglia' ('Battle Madonna') or 'Madonna della Vittoria' ('Madonna of Victory'), like the well-known—and potent—Virgins revered at Canossa and Mantua.

What little we know about the two battle murals indicates they were to have been at the tops of their respective walls. Leonardo's surface preparation that is reported to have gone bad was 'high up there', and Michelangelo's mural apparently was to have gone on a wall having a good deal of clear space over its remarkably low windows. Other important battle or tournament murals or fitted wall panels of the period usually were placed at the tops of the walls on which they were found.[154]

Neither of the two battle murals appears to have been planned to be very tall. Michelangelo drew his cartoon using a platform four *braccia* or 2.35m high, and his battle mural probably was meant to decorate a space no more than eight *braccia* or 4.7m high. Leonardo's battle mural likely was to have been at most 11 *braccia* or 6.4m high—that is, the maximum probable distance from the top of the *residenza* or tribune of the *Signoria* to the cornice beneath the ceiling, as well as the maximum distance from the possible ledge to the cornice.

If Leonardo's *Capture of a Standard* in fact was—or still is—no more than three metres high, was placed fairly low in the mural and was not planned to have anything important above it, the mural can hardly have been intended to be any more than 6.4m high.[155] In that case if, as the record implies, Leonardo used all of his initial supply of paper to assemble his cartoon, the length of his battle mural would have been at least 36.0m.[156] If we suppose that the height of Leonardo's battle mural was to have been equal to the height probably planned for Michelangelo's, that is, around 4.5m, we arrive at a length for it of at least 49.6m. This measurement is close to the length of the west wall, which was about 53m, and not far from the length of the east wall, which was about 62m.

Michelangelo almost certainly did not complete his cartoon.[157] The known amount of paper acquired for its assembly was around 113m² or slightly more.[158] If Michelangelo used all of and only this paper, it would have created an area of around 100m² or slightly larger. This would comprise, at most, only 45 percent of the area Leonardo apparently was preparing and therefore likely represents only a part of Michelangelo's projected work—how large a part we unfortunately cannot determine.

But perhaps we can form some idea of the choices Michelangelo, and the Florentine government, faced as he was planning his great battle mural. The well-known copy of the lost piece of cartoon showing the reactions of a group of bathing soldiers to a false alarm (Fig. 6) records the only scene for the mural that is now known with reasonable certainty. If it was in fact to have been about or nearly 4.5m high—that is, about 80–100cm taller than the scenes by Perugino, Botticelli and others on the walls of the Sistine Chapel in Rome and nearly the same height as Leonardo's *Last Supper* in Milan—its width would have been around 8.8m, as its proportions appear to have been about 1 to almost 2. Michelangelo could only place the successive scenes one alongside another. There was not enough room on the wall to stack scenes as tall as this; for even between and at the sides of the windows, the wall's paintable surface probably was no more than 14 *braccia* or 8.2m high. (Nor can one think of any stacked battle scenes among the other great murals of the period.)

Unlike Leonardo, Michelangelo often kept his scenes separate by framing them. What he may have been planning, then, was a frieze-like succession of clearly distinct scenes either all the same size or else alternating in width, rather like a giant *predella*. These scenes would have extended at least 22.2m and probably a great deal more across the west wall of the Great Hall, which was almost nine metres shorter than the east wall (it was around 53m long).[159]

Let us assume that the scenes themselves were to have taken up the full available height of perhaps 4.5m. (Because of the cornice at the top of the wall, there was no need for frames there; and whatever was to have gone between and at the sides of the windows may have made frames underneath the scenes unnecessary there also.)[160] Let us also assume that (painted) frames at least one *braccio* (58.4cm) wide were to have separated and flanked the several scenes. Let us finally assume that in order to end up with a picture instead of a piece of frame in the middle of the Hall, Michelangelo planned to use an odd number of scenes. Such a layout would have been similar to the one he later used on the Sistine Ceiling and the one Vasari used on the side walls of the Great Hall. It follows that, if Michelangelo was planning to use uniform scene sizes, a three-scene arrangement would have occupied around 28.8m (3 x 8.8m or slightly less + 4 x 0.6m or slightly more) and a five-scene arrangement approximately 47.6m.[161]

If on the other hand Michelangelo intended to alternate wide scenes (of which the first, the scene of the *Bathing Soldiers*, evidently was one) with others only half as wide,[162] then a five-scene arrangement would have occupied around 38.8m (3 x 8.8m or slightly less + 2 x 4.4m or slightly less + 6 x 0.6m or slightly more) and a seven-scene arrangement (with a small scene in the center, just as on the Sistine Ceiling or the walls of the Great Hall as we see them today) around 53.2m or the full length of the wall.

There thus is good reason to believe that the two battle murals were to have been long, frieze-like pictures or sequences of scenes, possibly running the entire length of the Great Hall.[163] This would explain why each artist prepared his cartoon elsewhere in an enormous space made available to him by the city: Leonardo in the Sala del Papa (Hall of the Pope) in the convent of Santa Maria Novella, and Michelangelo in the Sala dei Tintori (Hall of the Dyers) in the faraway convent of Sant'Onofrio.[164]

It is generally assumed that the two battle murals were planned to be the same size. But Leonardo's probably was to have been taller than Michelangelo's. Leonardo appears to have received far more paper than Michelangelo did. The paper he used was slightly more expensive and therefore possibly heavier. He apparently used far more paste per square metre to assemble his cartoon, indicating that it may have needed to be stronger in order to support its possibly greater height.[165]   Michelangelo was able to prepare his cartoon using two trestles or sawhorses four *braccia* or 2.35m high and some boards,[166] whereas Leonardo prepared his from a structure usually described as a *ponte* (literally: a 'bridge') and apparently costing several times as much.[167]

And perhaps most important: the size of the largest unobstructed rectangle that could be obtained at the top of the wall was considerably greater—in both height and length—on Leonardo's side of the Hall (the east one) than it was on the side on which Michelangelo evidently was to have worked.   On Leonardo's side the available rectangular space might have been as much as 6.4m high and was about 62m long; whereas on the west side, because of the windows, it probably was only between 4.1 and 4.7m high, and it was only about 53m long.[168]   In terms of area the available rectangular space on Leonardo's side might have been as much as $397m^2$, whereas on the west side it probably was only between 217 and $249m^2$.   In any case Leonardo's mural probably was to have been longer, as the wall on which he painted was almost nine metres longer than the one on which Michelangelo apparently was to have worked.

It remains possible the two battle murals were nevertheless to have been the same size—or at least had the same height.   For the figure of $217$-$249m^2$ just calculated for the largest probable unobstructed rectangular area on the west wall is not, after we allow for trimming, framing, considerable margins of error and other factors, appreciably different from the figure of $223m^2$ given previously for the smallest probable size of Leonardo's cartoon according to the recorded amounts of paper that were supplied for it.[169]

We do not, to be sure, know whether this recorded paper was all that Leonardo used or planned to use, or whether the area of the cartoon corresponded to the full area of his projected mural (or that section of it for which the cartoon was made).[170] It nevertheless is possible that the similarity of the figures for the available space at the top of the west wall and the probable size of Leonardo's cartoon is significant and indicates that Leonardo designed his cartoon to match, at least in height, the largest available rectangular space on the wall across from the one on which he was going to work.[171] If so, he obviously did so in the expectation that another mural would be painted in that space, creating, when both his and this other mural had been painted (did Leonardo first think he would be painting the other mural himself?), a more or less symmetrical arrangement similar in some ways to the one by Vasari that we see today.

It is probable indeed that both long walls of the Great Hall were to have been painted. For it should now be clear that Leonardo's cartoon either would have been taller than Michelangelo's, in which case Michelangelo's mural could hardly have been planned for the same wall; or else, if its height was the same, Leonardo's cartoon, even though it was destined to be reproduced on the east wall, would probably have fit perfectly into the available space over the windows in the west wall. In that case Leonardo must have expected the west wall to be painted as well as the east one. Either way, both walls were to have been painted. Were the two murals to have been different in height? Although we strongly suspect they were, we cannot give a definite answer to this question on the basis of our present knowledge. But if Leonardo's *Capture of a Standard*, or significant remnants of it, can be recovered, we should easily be able to determine this, as well as establish the overall height of his great projected battle mural.[172]

Most of the great monumental rooms of the Italian Late Middle Ages and Renaissance were completely decorated, mostly with paintings. Examples include the Sala delle Asse or Hall of the Boards in the Castello Sforzesco in Milan, with its ingenious but mostly lost paintings by Leonardo (the boards are lost also); and the Sistine and Pauline Chapels in the Vatican Palace in Rome, with their awesome and unsettling frescoes by Michelangelo. Other examples are the Sala della Ragione or Hall of Business in Padua (which enormous hall—in spite of what Vasari thought—is even larger than the one in Florence), the Sala del Maggior Consiglio or Hall of the Major Council in the Ducal Palace in Venice (to which great room we have referred before) and the Sala dei Dugento or Hall of the Two Hundred in Palazzo Vecchio in Florence (to which we have also referred and where tapestries were used instead of paintings). And in those rooms where only some walls were fully decorated, such as the refectory of the convent of Santa Maria delle Grazie in Milan, with its great *Last Supper* by Leonardo, the walls containing important paintings usually were the ones that were filled completely.[173]

One therefore wonders whether Leonardo and Michelangelo designed their battle murals to cover all of the paintable surfaces of their respective walls, from corner to corner and from cornice above to woodwork below. But from what little evidence we have, it appears that they did not plan their two battle murals to come down all the way to the woodwork of the Great Hall. There thus would have been spaces between the battle murals above and the woodwork below, as well perhaps as spaces at the sides of the murals.

Were these spaces simply to have been left empty, as they might be in a museum or a modern living room? Is it not likely that here too some form of decoration was envisioned? And is it not possible that the end walls of the Hall were expected to receive some kind of decoration also? Were other artists to have made these decorations? Were Leonardo and Michelangelo to have made them? We are unlikely ever to know.

It is worth noting, however, that every contemporary source save one states or implies that Leonardo and Michelangelo were going to *paint the Hall*—not 'paint in the Hall', not 'make paintings in the Hall'.[174] And the one exception, which is the agreement between Leonardo and the *Signoria*, speaks of Leonardo's obligation to paint 'a panel (or picture) of the Great Hall of the Council',[175] implying that other 'panels' or 'pictures' were to be painted also.

We must acknowledge the likelihood, therefore, that it was expected—or at least hoped—that Leonardo and Michelangelo were going to paint the entire Hall, or at least most of it. Already at the time, it was recognized that what they could be depended upon to produce would be supremely and uniquely great.[176] Even to imagine what the completed mural decorations of the Great Hall might have looked like is beyond the capabilities of most of us. But let us at least try to recapture what little of them we can.

**FIGURE 1.** Florence, Palazzo Vecchio, Salone dei Cinquecento, looking north (around 1900). A small piece of Vasari's *Battle of Marciano* is visible at the far right. This fresco, together with the 'incrustation' that supports it, probably covers the piece of wall on which Leonardo painted his *Capture of a Standard*.

**FIGURE 2.** Copy after the *Capture of a Standard* by Leonardo da Vinci (the 'Doria' copy); private collection.

**FIGURE 3.** Copy after the *Capture of a Standard* by Leonardo da Vinci (the 'Uffizi' copy); Florence, Museo di Palazzo Vecchio.

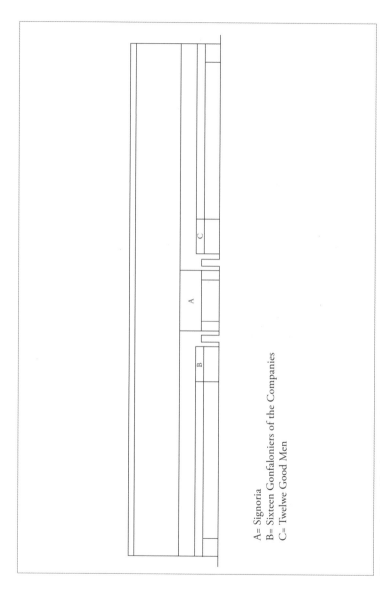

A = Signoria
B = Sixteen Gonfaloniers of the Companies
C = Twelve Good Men

FIGURE 4. Possible elevation of the east wall of the Great Hall as of 1505.

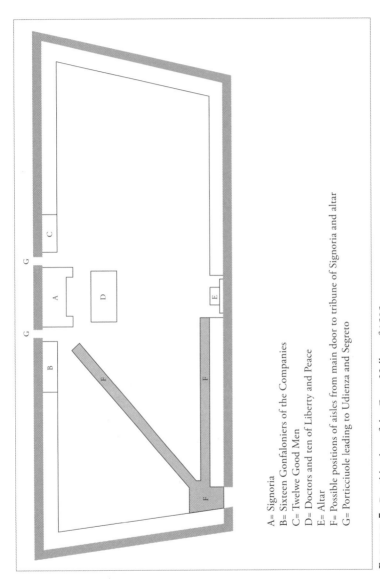

A= Signoria

B= Sixteen Gonfaloniers of the Companies

C= Twelwe Good Men

D= Doctors and ten of Liberty and Peace

E= Altar

F= Possible positions of aisles from main door to tribune of Signoria and altar

G= Porticciuole leading to Udienza and Segreto

FIGURE 5. Possible plan of the Great Hall as of 1505.

FIGURE 6. Aristotile da Sangallo, copy after the piece of cartoon by Michelangelo showing *Bathing Soldiers Reacting to a False Alarm*; Holkham Hall (Norfolk).

**FIGURE 7.** Leonardo da Vinci, *A Reserve Corps about to Go into Action* ('The Cavalcade'); Windsor, Royal Library.

**FIGURE 8.** Fra Bartolomeo, *Altarpiece of the Major Council*, Florence, Museo di San Marco.

# NOTES

1  B. Cerretani, *Ricordi*, ed. G. Berti (Istituto Nazionale di Studi sul Rinascimento, *Studi e testi, XXIX*), Florence, 1993, pp. 115–16: 'Im questo tempo Lionardo da Vincci, maestro grandissimo et fiorentino di pittura, cominc[i]ò a dipignere la Sala del Consiglio in quella faccia sopra dove stanno et [*sic*] 12 Buoni Huomini, et fessi amattonare quel'andito del Palazo in Sala con matoni quasi tonddi, et apichòsi in Sala detta nove bandiere toltte al signore Bart[olome]o d'Alviano più g[i]orni fa'. (Not printed in E. Villata, *Leonardo da Vinci: I documenti e le testimonianze contemporanee*, Milan, 1999.) Cerretani's *Ricordi* were rediscovered in the Vatican Library in the early 1990s.

2  For the time, see p. 36 at n. 108. Officially—but very rarely—the Council was called the Council of the People and Commune, that is, the single parliamentary body that replaced both previous major councils. On it see esp. N. Rubinstein, 'I primi anni del Consiglio Maggiore di Firenze', *Archivio Storico Italiano*, CXII, 1954, pp. 151–94 and pp. 321–47. The Hall was not normally known as the Hall of the Great Council, as it is often called in recent studies. It was sometimes used also for *Pratiche* (consultations involving selected leading citizens), meetings of the Council of the Eighty (which had to pass all proposed legislation before it could be taken before the Major Council), or even meetings of the *Signori e Collegi*, as well as 'exhibitions' and assemblies of the Florentine militia.

3  See n. 24. The 'venerable' *Collegi* (n.b.: the word originally meant 'colleges' [as it does in modern Italian], but in the early sixteenth century it was often used in the sense of 'colleagues') always deliberated together with the *Signoria* and did not have any executive responsibilities of their own. They did not have

their own quarters in the Palace, nor did they keep their own records. They did—at least in theory—perform some military or guard duties: the Sixteen commanded the 16 companies of the citizen militia (one for each of the city's wards), and the Twelve were responsible for the safety of the Palace. The *Signoria* could not initiate important legislation, take many financial measures, or make important appointments without the approval of both 'Colleges'. ('Signoria' is the collective name for the nine *Signori* who ruled the Republic; see n. 6.) Nor could either the Major Council or the Council of the Eighty act unless a quorum of both Colleges was present. During the plague of 1527 we hear of meetings of the Major Council's twice having to be cancelled because of the absences of two of the Twelve and two of the Sixteen respectively; Signori e Collegi, Deliberazioni in Forza di Ordinaria Autorità (henceforth: Deliberazioni), 129, fols. 163r and 167r. With one exception this and all other documents cited here are in the State Archives of Florence (Archivio di Stato di Firenze). On the Twelve see also Donato Giannotti, 'Discorso sopra il formare il governo di Firenze' (1527) and 'Discorso intorno alla forma della Repubblica di Firenze' (1529), in his *Opere politiche e letterarie*, ed. F.-L. Polidori, Florence, 1850, I, pp. 15 and 32.

4   He probably went there in June 1506. (The French had taken Milan from the Sforza family in 1499.) The diplomatic exchanges (all printed [with numerous errors] in Villata [as in n. 1], pp. 200–16, nos 233–49, passim), two of them signed by the king himself, make it perfectly clear that the French put considerable pressure on the (very reluctant) Florentine government to obtain Leonardo's services. The Florentine Republic relied heavily on France, especially in its efforts to recover Pisa, which Florence had lost when the Medici were expelled from it towards the end of 1494. In 1502 the Republic raised 60,000 gold florins (perhaps one fifth of its normal annual

budget) to subsidize the French king; Provvisioni, Registri (henceforth: Provvisioni), 193 (bobina 375), fols. 45r–47v. It continued to subsidize him heavily for at least the next five years; Camera del Comune, Depositario della Signoria, Giornali di Entrata e Uscita, 19, fol. 9r (1505); 16, fols. 87a-b; 24, fols. 146a-b; 25, fols. 149a-b (all 1506); and 2 (1507), fols. 14a-b (these records are far from complete). In 1509 the Republic sent two lion cubs to the French governor of Milan 'ad remunerationem innumerabilium beneficiorum collatorum civitati Florentie' ('in remuneration of the innumerable benefits bestowed upon the city of Florence'); Deliberazioni, 111, fol. 102v. Leonardo did *not* leave Florence out of 'indignation' or discouragement with his battle mural, as some of the sources would have us believe.

5     G. Vasari, *Le opere*, ed. G. Milanesi, Florence, 1906 (1973) (henceforth: Vasari-Milanesi or ed. Milanesi), IV, pp. 319–20; and VII, p. 159; and B. Cellini, *Vita*, I, xii (ed. E. Camesasca, Milan, 1985, p. 105).

6     The Gonfalonier of Justice was the leader of the *Signoria*. At the time with which we are concerned, he served for life. (His name was Piero di Messer Tommaso Soderini.) The other eight *Signori*, whose term lasted for only two months, were also known as Priors (of Liberty). The Sixteen Gonfaloniers of the Companies served for four months, the Twelve Good Men for three. The offices of the *Signori*, Sixteen, and Twelve were known collectively as the *Tre Maggiori* or 'Three Majors'. A Florentine *braccio* was about 0.584m.

7     In the early 1560s Giorgio Vasari, either on the advice or else with the approval of Michelangelo and acting on the orders of Duke Cosimo I de' Medici, raised the ceiling of the Hall by probably 12 *braccia* or 7.0m to a height, Vasari says, of 32 *braccia* or 18.7m in order to rectify the room's proportions

and provide better lighting; see U. Muccini, *The Salone dei Cinquecento of Palazzo Vecchio*, Florence, 1990, pp. 55–76; Vasari-Milanesi, IV, pp. 452–53; and n. 84. The Hall's original height, if the figure Vasari gives for its present height is correct, therefore would have been 20 *braccia* or 11.7m. In one place, however (VII, p. 700), Vasari says that he raised the ceiling by 13 *braccia* or 7.6m. If so, and if his figure for its present height is accurate, the Hall's original height would have been 19 *braccia* or 11.1m. Vasari also says (VI, p. 170) that the duke's *Udienza* (Audience Area) by the sculptor Baccio Bandinelli and others at the north end of the Hall (Fig. 1, middle) is 18 *braccia* (10.5m) tall but that it failed to reach all the way to the original ceiling. The *Udienza* therefore may have once come to the level at which the *cornicione* or cornice beneath the ceiling rested; on the *cornicione* see n. 81.

8    The *Signori e Collegi* could not have been at either end because: (1) there were windows in the middle of both end walls, one of them probably positioned at a height of 5 *braccia* or 2.9m (it is now at 2.8m) and the other almost certainly no higher than that, and the *residenza* (tribune or dais) of the *Signoria* probably was at least 8 *braccia* or 4.7m tall (see pp. 22 at n. 73; and 40 before n. 121; and nn. 128 and 130); (2) the end walls are both external walls facing public spaces (Piazza della Signoria on the north and what today is called Via della Ninna on the south), and two *porticciuole* or 'small doors' are known to have led to rooms or apartments behind the *Signori e Collegi* (see p. 9 at n. 23); (3) the two *anditi* (passageways or aisles) leading from the main door to the altar and to the *residenza* of the *Signoria* respectively, and about which we read in a document of 1498 (see p. 14, paragraph following n. 47; and Fig. 5), would have made little sense if the *Signori e Collegi* had sat before one of the end walls; (4) the Doctors of Law and the Ten of Liberty and Peace could hardly have been seated in front of both the

altar and the *Signori* if the *Signori* had sat before one of the end walls (see n. 97); (5) Leonardo's enormous battle mural could hardly have been destined for a wall consisting in great part of windows (see p. 40 before n. 121; and n. 128); and (6) neither end wall was large enough to contain this mural, if we assume that it was to have covered an area at least approaching 223 square metres (see p. 44 at n. 138).

9    Vasari-Milanesi, IV, p. 450: 'e nel mezzo della facciata che è volta a levante era una residenza più eminente, dove col Confaloniere di Iustizia stavano i Signori; e da ciascun lato di questo più eminente luogo erano due porte, una delle quali entrava nel Segreto e l'altra nello Specchio; e nella facciata che è dirimpetto a questa dal lato di ponente, era un altare . . .' ('and in the middle of the wall [*literally*: facade] that is turned to the east was a *residenza* [tribune or dais] that was more eminent [scil., *higher than the* ringhiera *or gallery occupied by the other magistrates*; for it see the beginning of p. 18], where the *Signori* sat with the Gonfalonier of Justice, and at either side of this more eminent place were two doors, one of which entered the *Segreto* and the other the *Specchio*; and on the wall that is across from this one on the west side was an altar . . .'). None of the extensive information that Vasari gives on the Hall is found in his first edition, which was published before he began working there around 1560; see G. Vasari, *Le vite de' più eccellenti pittori, scultori e architettori nelle redazioni del 1550 e 1568*, ed. R. Bettarini and P. Barocchi, Florence, 1976, IV, pp. 241–42.

10    H. T. Newton and J. Spencer, 'On the Location of Leonardo's *Battle of Anghiari*', *Art Bulletin*, LXIV, 1982, pp. 47–48. This study is the most recent of the three of which I know that seriously attempt to ascertain the position and size of the mural. The others, which also consider the position and size of the battle mural by Michelangelo, are those of Johannes Wilde

(see p. 41 at n. 126) and Christian-Adolf Isermeyer (see the beginning of p. 44). Neither Wilde nor Isermeyer considers the possibility of relocating Leonardo's famous painting.

11    N. Rubinstein, *The Palazzo Vecchio, 1298-1532* (*Oxford-Warburg Studies*), Oxford, 1995, p. 41 and esp. pp. 114–15.

12    One cannot use Vasari to prove that the *Signori* (*e Collegi*) sat before the west wall. He says, quite unmistakably, that they sat before the east wall. See the passage cited in n. 9, in which he states that the chapel across from the *Signori* was 'dal lato di ponente (*west*)' and that the *Signori* sat in the middle of the 'facciata che è volta a levante' ('wall that is turned to the east'). Using the same figure of speech, he later describes the duke's *Udienza* by Bandinelli and others (Fig. 1, middle) as being 'in quella testa che è volta a tramontana' ('at that end which is turned to the north'; VI, p. 170); the *Udienza* in fact is at the north end of the Hall. Rubinstein's main point is that, as the main door was then in the Hall's northwest corner (see p. 15 at n. 48; and Fig. 5), the *Signori* would have had to cross the Hall on their way to their seats if their tribune was located on its eastern side. But the *Signori* had to cross a good deal of Hall no matter which side they sat on, as the door from which they entered it was in a corner. That is why a passageway or aisle was built from this door to the tribune of the *Signoria* in 1497–98 (see p. 14, paragraph following n. 47). If the *Signori e Collegi* had sat before the west wall, the Sixteen Gonfaloniers of the Companies, who, as a document of 1504 clearly appears to inform us, were seated in the northern half of the Hall (ibid.), would have been at the proper left of the *Signori*. But in fact the Sixteen, because of their great antiquity and prestige, must have been at the proper right of the *Signori* (see p. 13 at n. 44), who therefore are unlikely to have sat before the west wall (see also pp. 10–12 beginning at n. 32). It is clear, then, that there were other considerations, such as the impossibility of attaching impor-

tant ancillary structures—or a special means of access for the *Signori*—to the outside of the Hall in the middle of its western side (see below), that outweighed the relatively minor and in any case insoluble inconvenience to which Rubinstein draws attention.

13  Operai di Palazzo, 8, fols. 107r (1498): 'per dua fregi di marmj rossi per le porticciuole et per libbre 1620 [*550.8kg or about 196.7dm³*] di marmo rosso per le sogl[i]e' ('for two friezes of red marble for the little doors and for 1620 pounds of red marble for the doorsills'); 111r (printed in n. 24); and 123r (1499): 'A Giulio (?) scharpellino, cioè di Sandro, per opere 18 lavorò alle porticciuole della Sala' ('To Giulio [?] the stonecutter, that is, Giulio [?] di Sandro, for 18 days he worked on the little doors of the Hall'); and 10, fols. 74r: 'per un pezo di marmo rosso per fare una cornice all'uscio del Segreto del Consigl[i]o di libbre 430 [*146.2kg or about 52.2dm³*]' (for a piece of red marble of 430 pounds to make a cornice for the door of the *Segreto* of the Council'); and 74v (both 1505): 'la cornice del marmo rosso alla porta de[l] Segreto del Consigl[i]o' ('the cornice of red marble on the door of the *Segreto* of the Council'). (All previously uncited.)

14  Camera dell'Arme, Repubblicana (henceforth: Camera dell'Arme), 15 (1505), fol. 4r: 'le finestre della Sala del Consiglio sopra alla residenza della Signoria' ('the windows of the Hall of the Council over the *residenza* [tribune] of the *Signoria*'). (Printed more fully in n. 46; on the elimination of these windows around the end of 1504, see there.) Also Operai di Palazzo, 10, fol. 40v (1502): 'un pezo di finestra in decta Sala sopra al capo de' Dodici' ('a piece of window in the said Hall over the head of the Twelve'). (Both documents previously uncited.) See Vasari's description (cited in n. 9).

15  As is pointed out by J. Wilde, 'The Hall of the Great Council of Florence', *Journal of the Warburg and Courtauld Institutes*,

VII, 1944, p. 65; and Rubinstein, *Palazzo Vecchio*, p. 114. The decision to convert the Hall was made only in late November; Deliberazioni, 114, fol. 125v (cited in n. 17).

16    K. Frey, 'Studien zu Michelagniolo Buonarroti und zur Kunst seiner Zeit', *Jahrbuch der königlich preussischen Kunstsammlungen*, XXX, 1909, Beiheft, pp. 115–29 (1496–1503), passim (plus a good deal more that Frey omitted); for the frame for the altarpiece see p. 125, nos. 126–27. The diarist Luca Landucci regarded the removal of this woodwork as a great loss to his city; *Diario fiorentino*, ed. I. del Badia, Florence, 1883, p. 333 (1512): 'la qual cosa dolse a tutto Firenze—non la mutazione dello stato ma quella bella opera del legniame di tanta spesa. Ed era di grande riputazione ed onore della città avere sì bella residenza. Quando veniva una anbasceria a vicitare la Signoria, facieva stupire chi la vedeva, quando entravono in sì magna residenza e in sì grande cospetto di Consiglio de' cittadini' ('the which thing grieved all Florence—not the change in government but that beautiful woodwork that had cost so much. And it was to the city's great reputation and honour to have such a beautiful meeting place. When an embassy came to visit the *Signoria*, it stupified whoever saw it when they entered into such a great meeting place and into so great a presence of Council of the citizens').

17    Deliberazioni, 114, fol. 125v (22 November 1512): 'Deliberaverunt . . . precipi Operarijs Sancte Marie Floris de Florentia quatenus dent et tradant Baccino Angelj architectori et Caput Magistro Palatij dictorum Dominorum omnia ligniamina que fuerint opus pro sala dicti Palatij reactanda que vocabatur Sala Consilij Maioris . . .' ('They decided . . . that the *Operai* [Works Commissioners] of Santa Maria del Fiore [*scil.: the Cathedral*] of Florence are to be ordered to give and hand over to Baccino

[*scil.: 'Little Baccio'*] d'Agnolo, architect and *Capomaestro* of the Palace of the said *Signori*, all the wood that may be necessary to renovate the hall of the said Palace that was called the Hall of the Major Council'). (Previously uncited.)

18   Baccio was *Capomaestro* (chief architect, foreman) of the *Opera* (Works Commission) of the Palace from 24 May 1498 until after 27 October 1532—with one brief interruption in 1500–1, when he was suspected of peculation, and another in 1503, during which very short time he was replaced by the architect Giuliano da Sangallo. Operai di Palazzo, 8, fol. 26r-v (1499); 9, fols. 3v–4r and 29r-v (1500 and 1501); 12, fol. 36r (1503); and 15, fol. 27r (1532), etc. He thus was responsible also for the second dismantling of the Hall, which was carried out by the Palace carpenter, Antonio Buttasassi. This second removal of the woodwork was completed by 15 October 1530. Between 20 October and 15 November of that year there followed the construction in the Hall of 15 rooms of wood, four of masonry, and one containing a spiral staircase, in which up to 312 mattresses were placed and costing, with their beds and tables, around 6932 silver *lire* or *lire di piccioli* (989 gold florins), for the soldiers who now again guarded the Palace and controlled the city. The Sala del Papa (see n. 164) also was prepared to accommodate soldiers but not used. Operai di Palazzo, 15, fol. 22r-v (1531); Signori e Collegi, Condotte e Stanziamenti (henceforth: Condotte e Stanziamenti), 30 (1530–35), fols. 80v–83r, passim; and Otto di Pratica, Deliberazioni, Condotte e Stanziamenti, 15 (1529–31), fols. 71r–74v, passim.

19   All we know about the restoration as such is that well over 2000 gold florins (14,000 silver *lire*) probably were spent on it; Condotte e Stanziamenti, 27, fols. 251r, 255v and 266v (January, May and December 1528). The sum originally appropriated for the Hall's construction was 3000 *fiorini di grossi* (about 2500

gold florins) to be spent over a period of 18 months, plus the income from the pardons that the *Operai* were empowered to grant to certain tax debtors and to most criminals condemned by the *Otto di Guardia* (Eight of Safety) during the previous ten years. Provvisioni, 186 (bobina 369), fols. 109v–110v (1495). (All documents in this note previously uncited.)

20  Balìe, 44 (1512–27), fol. 489r: 'Et possasi et debbasi ragunare decto Consiglio decto dì 21 [di maggio 1527] al suono della campana grossa et rintochi di quella; et Il numero sufficiente sia 800 almeno delli habilj al decto Consiglio, Ragunandosi nella Sala Maggiore dove si soleva ragunare, La quale si rassettj et riduca per li Operaj del Palagio nel modo che stava prima. Et decto dì, inanzi che si cominci a fare alchuna altra cosa, si canti una messa dello Spirito Sancto al nome di Dio et della sancta Trinità et a buono et felice principio di tal Consiglio et conservatione di quello' ('And the said Council may and must convene on the said 21st day [of May 1527] at the sound of the great bell and its toll; and the sufficient number will be at least 800 of those eligible for the said Council, convening in the Major Hall where it used to convene, which [Hall] shall be repaired and brought back by the *Operai* of the Palace to the way it was before. And the said day, before any other thing is begun, there shall be sung a Mass of the Holy Ghost in the name of God and of the Holy Trinity and for the good and felicitous beginning of the same Council and its preservation'). (Previously uncited.)

21  At least much of the woodwork was not demolished in 1512. Cerretani (as in n. 1), p. 295 (November-December 1512), says: 'Trassono dalla Loggia la ghuardia [scil., *the soldiers who now guarded the Palace and controlled the city*] e messola nella Sala del Consiglio, dove, cavatone le panche e mandatole in varii luoghi, feciono molte case d'abeto . . .' ('They withdrew the Guard from the Loggia [*scil., the Log-*

*gia della Signoria, now known as the Loggia dei Lanzi*] and put them in the Hall of the Council, where, having taken out the benches and had them taken to various places, they made many abodes of fir wood . . .'). The altar or 'chapel' clearly had been reinstalled or remade by 29 March 1529. That is when the *Signoria* ordered Fra Bartolomeo's (unfinished) 'egregia tabula Consilij Maius [sic]' ('outstanding altarpiece of the Major Council'; Fig. 8) to be placed on or in it; Deliberazioni, 131, fol. 58r.

22   In one place he says he was in Florence for four months, but in another he says he was there for two years; Vasari-Milanesi, VII, pp. 9 and 652. That Vasari indeed saw the Hall at this time (he was still in his teens) seems likely in view of the fact that he describes it as having contained Fra Bartolomeo's *Altarpiece of the Major Council* (ed. Milanesi, IV, p. 450). Even though unfinished (it is just a monochrome underpainting that Fra Bartolomeo abandoned in 1512, when the Medici abolished the Major Council), the altarpiece nevertheless stood in the Hall from early April 1529 until October 1530, when it was moved to the old council hall. See previous note; and Condotte e Stanziamenti, 30, fols. 80v–81r. The Hall must have been easily accessible. The text of all legislation to be proposed to the Council had to be posted there at least three days before being put to vote in order that any interested parties might be fully informed about it; Provvisioni, 186 (bobina 369), fols. 138v–139v (1495). Even if Vasari did not see the Hall during the period of the Last Republic, he clearly is very well informed about its appearance during that time.

23   Two obvious differences were that neither the *Altarpiece of the Major Council* (begun 1510) nor a large door in the southwest corner (begun 1507 or later) had been there when Leonardo had worked in the Hall. See the two preceding notes; and n. 49.

24  Operai di Palazzo, 8, fol. 111r (1498): 'due fregi di marmo rosso lavoratj, che nell'uno è scripto "Audientia", nell'altro "Segreto", per le porticiuole alla Sala Grande tra Signori e Collegi . . .' ('two friezes worked in red marble, in one of which is written "Audientia", in the other "Segreto", for the little doors in the Great Hall between the *Signori* and *Collegi* . . .'). Also Deliberazioni, 113 (1511), fol. 230v. (Both previously uncited.) See also n. 13. Vasari therefore was wrong when he identified the space behind one of the two doors as that of the *Specchio* (see n. 9). Evidently the inscription reading 'AUDIENTIA' was no longer visible when he wrote about the doors. The office of the *Specchio*, in which records were kept listing the eligible men who were behind in their tax payments and therefore usually disqualified from holding public office, was located, as Rubinstein shows (*Palazzo Vecchio*, pp. 88 and 110), between the offices of the *Prestanze* (direct taxes) and the *Grascia* (grain and livestock) on the site of what is now the part of Palazzo Vecchio facing Via de' Gondi.

25  In one record we read of both *porticciuole* leading to the *Segreto*; Operai di Palazzo, 8, fol. 8v (1498): 'illas duas porticciuolas Secretj' ('those two little doors of the *Segreto*'). Frey (as in n. 16), p. 120, no. 59, gives 'illos duos porticciuolos secretos' ('those two little secret harbors')! Councilmen drawn to be 'electioners' entered the *Segreto* to submit their nominations and then returned to a different seating area in the Hall; Provvisioni, 187 (bobina 370), fols. 36v–38r. They likely entered by one 'little door' and returned by the other. Before their own office was ready, the *Operai* often met in the Old Hall either 'in audientia Secretj Sale Consilij' ('in the audience chamber of the *Segreto* of the Hall of the Council'; Operai di Palazzo, 6, fols. 16r, 19r, and 25v [1496]); or else 'in Audientia et Secreto Sale Consilij' ('in the Audience Chamber and *Segreto* of the Hall of the Council'; fol. 18v). Clearly, the *Segreto* and *Udienza* there

were either different parts of the same space or else the same thing. See also the following note.

26 Three others were the *Segreto* of the old council hall today known as the Sala dei Dugento (Hall of the Two Hundred), that of the Sala dei Gigli (Hall of the Lilies) and that of the Room of the Secretaries. The *Segreto* of the Old Hall was a part of that room which had been partitioned off into what was sometimes called a *recessus*; Rubinstein, *Palazzo Vecchio*, p. 109. But the *Segreto* of the Great Hall clearly was a separate room or suite of rooms (see below), and the doorway leading to it clearly was part of a wall, as it was at least partly framed with marble (see p. 8 at n. 13). The *Segreto* of the Sala dei Gigli (Sala Grande de' Signori) is mentioned in Operai di Palazzo, 10, fol. 15v (1501). It evidently was a separate space also. The *Segreto* of the Room of the Secretaries, which may not yet have existed when Leonardo worked in the Great Hall, had a *desco* (desk or table) 4½ *braccia* or 2.6m long; Deliberazioni, 114 (1512), fol. 237r.

27 Electoral procedures involving the *Segreto* of the Great Hall are set forth in, for example, Provvisioni, 186 (bobina 369), fols. 140r–142r (November 1495); and 187 (bobina 370), fols. 36r–38r (June 1496); as well as Signori e Collegi, Deliberazioni in Forza di Speciale Autorità, 39, fols. 19v–20r (June 1496). See also Rubinstein, 'Primi anni' (as in n. 2), esp. pp. 331–32, n. 226.

28 Operai di Palazzo, 8, fol. 129r (1499); and 10, fols. 7v and 51v (1500 and 1503).

29 Camera dell'Arme, 21, fol. 15v; and 40, fol. 16b.

30 Operai di Palazzo, 8, fols. 131r and 140r (1499 and 1500); and 10, fol. 26r (1502); and Camera dell'Arme, 38 (1509), fol. 16b.

31  Operai di Palazzo, 10, fol. 81v (July-August 1505): 'il palco del maghazino drento el Segreto' ('the floor of the store room in the *Segreto*').

32.  Ibid., fols. 80v–81v. The *magazzino* appears to have been at least 7.0m long. Its two *palchi* or floors had planks of 12 *braccia*, and at least 2000 *mezzane* were used to pave these *palchi*. As a rule, 21 old *mezzane* sufficed to cover a square metre; see p. 28 at n. 85. (At least one of the *palchi* probably had two layers of *mezzane*: one for the flooring and the other to support the flooring.) The staircase was 8 *braccia* or 4.7m long. The *Segreto* of the Old Hall also was a respectable space, having benches with 50 square *braccia* (17.1m$^2$) of wainscotting (by the sculptor and woodworker Benedetto da Maiano) behind them and requiring a good deal of green cloth to cover its desks and tables; Operai di Palazzo, 2, fols. 1v and 49r (both 1478); and Camera dell'Arme, 21 (1512), fol. 25v.

33  Operai di Palazzo, 6, fol. 57v: 'ab archalibus fenestrarum Sale Nove Magne usque in terram super lastricho Dogane' ('from the arches of the windows of the Great New Hall all the way to the ground on the pavement of the [Corte della] Dogana [(Courtyard of the) Customs House]'). The Dogana had been begun around 1445; Rubinstein, *Palazzo Vecchio*, p. 25. Before its construction the open space behind the Palace had been known as the Corte (or Cortile) del Capitano.

34  That the Corte della Dogana was on the side facing the Palace is clear from the fact that the space in question is sometimes called 'Cortile della Dogana' to this day as well as from a previously uncited document of May 1499, in which we read of a workman who 'chascò in terra in Dogana dal palchetto haveva facto al muro del Palagio per ronperlo et raconciare e doccionj dell'aquaio della cucina de' Signorj . . .' ('fell to the ground in

the [Corte della] Dogana from the scaffolding he had made on the wall of the Palace in order to break through it and repair the drainpipes of the sink of the kitchen of the *Signori* . . .'); Operai di Palazzo, 8, fol. 123v (also fol. 27r [January 1499]). The word 'Dogana' often signifies the courtyard between the building of that name and the Palace rather than the building itself. For example: 'braccia 45 di schagl[i]onj misuratj che sono nella Corte di Dogana . . . et braccia 98½ di listre che braccia 45½ sono murate et resto sono in Dogana' ('45 *braccia* of measured steps that are in the Corte di Dogana . . . and 98½ *braccia* of [stone] strips of which 45½ *braccia* have been built in and the rest are in the [Corte di] Dogana'); ibid., fol. 109v (1498). Also: 'per dipintura della prospectiva della finestra di saletta dal camino . . . che riesce ~~in Dogana~~ [*crossed out*] nella corte del Palagio' ('for painting the "perspective" of the window of the room of the fireplace . . . that opens onto the courtyard of ~~the Dogana~~ the Palace'); Operai di Palazzo, 10, fol. 58r (1503). See also n. 38; and the first two documents cited in n. 46. On the construction of the windows in the side walls only after the rest of the Hall had been built, see p. 40 before n. 121.

35   Cf. n. 14: 'le finestre della Sala del Consiglio sopra alla residenza della Signoria' ('the windows of the Hall of the Council over the *residenza* [tribune] of the *Signoria*'). These were walled up around the end of 1504; see n. 46. Also: 'un pezo di finestra . . . sopra al capo de' Dodici' ('a piece of window . . . over the head of the Twelve'). This last *finestra* must have been one of the same windows, which according to Vasari were two; in any case, the window 'over the head' of the Twelve in all probability no longer existed when Leonardo began to paint. As the *Udienza* apparently was considered to be a part of the *Segreto* (see p. 10 at n. 24), these two spaces evidently were connected. It is therefore unlikely that there was any exterior wall directly behind the *Signoria*. See Figs. 4 and 5.

36  My thanks to Maurizio Seracini for reminding me about the earlier stairway. No evidence has ever come to light that two relatively small doors, probably around 13 or 14 *braccia* (7.6 or 8.2m) apart (see n. 96), once existed in the middle of the west wall, which has been investigated quite thoroughly; or that other walls were once attached to the outside of its lower middle; or that at least two windows once existed in its upper middle. The four seemingly functionless piers to which Newton and Spencer (as in n. 10), p. 48, draw attention are not situated near the middle of the Hall and therefore did not support the *Segreto* and *Udienza*, as Newton and Spencer thought possible.

37  See also n. 12.

38  Vasari-Milanesi, IV, p. 450; and Operai di Palazzo, 10, fol. 62r-v (1504): 'per segare 4 finestre della Sala del Consigl[i]o Grande dalla parte di Dogana' ('to saw 4 windows of the Great Hall of the Council on the side of the [Corte della] Dogana [(Courtyard of the) Customs House]'). On the height from the present floor at which the west windows were placed, see Newton and Spencer, p. 50. Maurizio Seracini believes that the positions of some of the west windows were different from the ones given in the diagram reproduced there but confirms that they were all placed at a height from the present floor of 1.7m.

39  That is, at least as high as the level of the *listre* or stone strips on which the frames containing Vasari's frescoes now rest. See pp. 22–23 after n. 73.

40  Ibid. No evidence of windows came to light when the plaster was removed in 1978 from all of the east wall beneath Vasari's frescoes and their frames, the stone strips underneath which rest at a level of 8 *braccia* or 4.7m. Nor did any windows come to light when thermography was performed in the same area a few years later. On the walling up of the east windows, see

n. 46 below. The place where the *Segreto*, *Udienza*, and *magazzino* evidently once were, is now occupied mostly by a staircase. One imagines that it was on the outside of the east wall that the frequently mentioned *necessari* or *agiamenti* (latrines), of which there probably were two, were located also; see, for example, Frey (as in n. 16), p. 127, nos. 136 and 137 (both 1502); and p.129, no. 159 (1504); also Operai di Palazzo, 6, fol. 67v (1497); and 8, fol. 131r (1499); and Camera dell'Arme, 38 (1509), fol. 16b.

41   For the years in which these offices were instituted, I am following Rubinstein, *Palazzo Vecchio*, pp. 10 and 19.

42   I am taking this information about the Sixteen and their inauguration mostly from the records of the *Camera del Comune* and the *Camera dell'Arme*, which paid for all or most of the government's ceremonies. See also Giannotti (as in n. 3), I, pp. 29–32.

43   According to Michelangelo's friend Benedetto Varchi, who was a noted historian (*Storia fiorentina*, ed. L. Arbib, Florence, 1843, I, pp. 220–21), the Sixteen were 'dopo la Signoria il primo e più nobile magistrato di Firenze, e dopo questo i Dodici Buonuomini' ('after the *Signoria* the first and most noble magistracy of Florence, and after that the Twelve Good Men'). When the republican constitution was abolished in 1532, both the *Signori* and the Sixteen were eliminated forever. But the Twelve were permitted to continue for centuries. (After 1532 they were usually called the 'Collegi' ['Colleagues'].) When in November of 1512 the *Signori e Collegi* were awarded salaries in place of the one that had previously been given to the Gonfalonier-for-life, Piero Soderini, who was now in exile, the Sixteen were given five gold florins each a month but the Twelve only four; Giovanni Cambi, *Istorie*, in *Delizie degli eruditi to-*

*scani*, ed. I. di San Luigi, Florence, XXI, 1786, p. 312. For the Secretary of the Ten of Liberty and Peace, Donato Giannotti, who was also a political theorist and a friend of Michelangelo, the Sixteen were the (only) *Collegi*, whom he evidently thought of, as did most others in the late 1520s, as individuals (colleagues) rather than groups ('colleges'); see Giannotti, I, pp. 17–42, passim (on the Twelve, whom Giannotti considered useless, see pp. 15 and 32). On the fifteenth day of each Signoria, one of the Sixteen 'protested', that is, urged in an oration, the Podestà and the other members of the Council of Justice, all of whom were foreigners, to perform their duties conscientiously; Deliberazioni, 106–14 (1504–12), passim; and Giannotti, I, pp. 31–32. None of the Twelve took part in any comparable observance.

44   The few descriptions of which I know of the seating arrangements of the *Signori e Collegi* do not say on which side the Twelve sat and once have the *Collegi* sitting at the feet of the *Signori* (see Rubinstein, *Palazzo Vecchio*, p. 112). That clearly was not the case in the Great Hall, where the *Collegi* were separated from the *Signori* by *porticciuole* or 'small doors'; see text following.

45   The chronicler Giovanni Cambi (in *Delizie* [as in n. 43], XXI, p. 65) relates that Lorenzo de' Medici made a point of keeping older citizens at his right when he was escorting them.

46   Camera dell'Arme, 15 (1504–5), fol. 4r: 'Francesco di Giovannj di Grazino (?) charetaio de' avere adì 29 di novembre [1504] £ dua, ß xvj, d. 4; sono per charetate 23 di sassj rechatj in Doghana dal Palagio del Podestà per rimurare le finestre della Sala del Consiglio sopra alla residenza della Signoria . . .' ('Francesco di Giovanni di Grazino [?], carter, is to receive on the 29th day of November [1504] two *lire*, 16 *soldi*, 4 *denari*; this sum is for 23 cartloads of stones taken to the [Corte della]

Dogana [(Courtyard of the) Customs House] from the Palace of the Podestà to wall up the windows of the Hall of the Council over the *residenza* [tribune] of the *Signoria*'). Also Operai di Palazzo, 10, fol. 71v (November-December 1504): 'A Francesco di Giovannj di Rinzino per carrettate 23 di sassi portati dal Palagio del Podestà in Dogana a ß2, d. 6 la carrectata . . . £2, ß16, d. 4' ('To Francesco di Giovanni di Rinzino for 23 cartloads of stones taken from the Palace of the Podestà to the [Corte della] Dogana at 2 *soldi*, 6 *denari* per cartload . . . £2, s. 16, d. 4'). The stones in question came from an abandoned staircase in the courtyard of the residence of the *Podestà*, the foreign official who was the city's supreme justice in non-commercial matters; the building is now known as the (Palazzo del) Bargello. Ibid.: 'per . . . havere fornito di disfare una scala vechia [nella Corte del Podestà] et portare fuora sassi et per mandargli nella Sala del Consigl[i]o' ('for having finished demolishing an old staircase [in the Courtyard of the *Podestà*] and to take out stones and for having them taken to the Hall of the Council'). (All three documents previously uncited.) A *carrettata* was the load that could be hauled in a *carretta*, a two-wheeled vehicle drawn by a single animal. To judge from the quantity of stones delivered, as well as the limited amount of space over the *residenza* of the *Signori*, the windows in question cannot have been very large (they certainly were not much more than 4.5m tall). See also n. 14; p. 11 at n. 38; and the beginning of p. 32. On the construction of the windows in the side walls only after the rest of the Hall had been built, see p. 40 before n. 121.

47 Ibid.; and n. 128.

48 Operai di Palazzo, 10, fol. 59v: 'braccia 28½ di panche fatte per l'andito della Sala del Consigl[i]o Grande dirinpetto a' Gonfalonierj'. Cf. Operai di Palazzo, 8, fol. 8v (1498): 'duorum

andarum [sic] ab porta Palatij usque ad altare et ad residentiam Dominorum' ('of the two passageways from the door of the Palace to the altar and to the *residenza* [tribune] of the *Signori*'); and 'le dua panche, cioè dall'altare et dalla residentia de' Signorj insino alla porta del Palazo' ('the two benches, that is, from the altar and from the *residenza* of the *Signori* to the door of the Palace'). The passageway leading to the *residenza* may have run diagonally as in our Fig. 5, or it may have skirted the north wall and the northern half of the east one in front of the *ringhiera* or magistrates' gallery that went all around the Hall (on it see the beginning of p. 18). The fact that the altar is named before the *residenza* in both entries leads one to picture it, as Wilde does (as in n. 15), p. 74, as being closer to the door to the Palace and therefore on the west side of the Hall. Wilde, however, supposes that one passageway led from this door to the altar and the other from the altar to the *residenza*. This seems most unlikely in view of both the wording and the facts that the Doctors of Law and the Ten of Liberty and Peace or of *Balìa*, as well, probably, as the *banditori* (criers or announcers), were seated between the altar and the *residenza*, and that there was also a *banco* (table, counter) with an electoral urn there; see n. 97.

49  This position would have or would put Leonardo's *Capture* across from the place now occupied by Vasari's *Rout of San Vincenzo*, which is the fresco by Vasari that most resembles it. (One might even call the middle part of Vasari's fresco a paraphrase of Leonardo's great painting.) Vasari painted the *Rout of San Vincenzo* in 1569; Muccini (as in n. 7), p. 133. He built the 'incrustation' or counterwall in front of Leonardo's scene (or the place where it had been) only around the end of 1570; see n. 85. He therefore might have had a clear view of the scene—provided it had not already been destroyed and was not concealed under whitewash or plaster—across from him while he was painting the *Rout of San Vincenzo*. More possible

confirmation that the Twelve sat before the right or southern half of the east wall is found in these directions sent to a friend by the writer Anton Francesco Doni, who was a friend of Michelangelo, in 1549: 'e salito le scale della Sala Grande, diligentemente date una vista a un gruppo di cavalli e d'uomini. . . di Lionardo da Vinci . . .' ('and having climbed the stairs of the Great Hall, diligently take a look at a group of horses and men . . . by Leonardo da Vinci . . .'), implying that Leonardo's scene will be more or less in front of him when he walks into the room after having gone up the stairs; see n. 102. In Doni's day the main entrance to the Hall was at the southern end of the west wall, at the head of the staircase (which no longer exists) built by the architect Cronaca from 1507 to 1510, about where the door to the Studiolo of Francesco I is now.

50  Operai di Palazzo, 8, fol. 63r (1500): 'Supradicti Operarij . . . declaraverunt Bartholomeum Angeli legnaiuolum, Capudmagistrum Opere Palatij, creditorem . . . librarum centum octuaginta *piccioli* . . . pro brachijs xij cornicionis, fregij et architravis factis in et ad dictam Residentiam ad rationem librarum xv *piccioli* pro quolibet brachio' ('The aforesaid *Operai* [Works Commissioners] . . . declared Bartolomeo [*nickname:* 'Baccio'] d'Agnolo the woodworker, *Capomaestro* of the *Opera* of the Palace, to be their creditor . . . for one hundred eighty *lire di piccioli* . . . for 12 *braccia* of cornice, frieze and architrave made on and for the said *residenza* at the rate of 15 *lire di piccioli* for each *braccio*'). The cornice, frieze and architrave were partly gilded (fol. 140v [1500]). The *Signori* probably sat in seats or stalls rather than on benches. In the Sala dell'Udienza they sat in *sederi*; Operai di Palazzo, 10, fol. 5v (1500): 'per aconciatura di più buche fe' rimurare nella Audientia de' nostrj Signorj quando si rifece e sederj de' decti Signorj' ('for fixing several holes he caused to be walled up in the Audience Chamber of our *Signori* when the seats of the said *Signori* were remade').

51 See n. 14. For the frieze and cornice see nn. 13 and 24. The entrance to the Chapel of the *Signoria* from the rooms of the Priors is described as a *porticciuola* in two documents of 1501; Operai di Palazzo, 10, fols. 23v and 24r. That doorway is about 88cm (1½ *braccia*) wide (about 117cm [2 *braccia*] with the jambs). But the *porticciuola* leading to the *Udienza* or the *Segreto* may have been somewhat larger. Surely it cannot have been too small if its 'cornice' (as distinct from its 'frieze') was made from a piece of marble weighing 146.2kg and therefore measuring about 52.2dm$^3$, and its doorsill from another weighing about 275.4kg and measuring about 98.4dm$^3$ (see n. 13).

52 Maurizio Seracini believes he has identified part of the arch of the (a) window some metres to the right or south of the east wall's present decorative centre; see pp. 31–32 beginning at n. 96. But in order to know exactly where this wall's historic centre was, we need to have the positions of both (or all) of the east windows or else those of the *porticciuole* or 'little doors'. On where one of these probably once was, see n. 96.

53 The physical centres of the side walls are not, and never were, in line with each other, nor are the side walls perfectly parallel. Because of the changes that Bandinelli, Vasari and others made in the end walls, the physical centre of the east wall might now be in a slightly different position from where it was during the Florentine Republic; see n. 54. For the ceiling and its *tondo* or round painting, see Frey (as in n. 16) pp. 115–16, no. 17; pp. 116–17, no. 25 (both 1496); p. 120, nos. 59 and 66; and p. 121, nos. 69 and 71 (all 1498). (There is a good deal more that Frey omitted.)

54 By 'decorative centre' of the east wall we mean the middle of the central (narrow) fresco by Vasari there (Fig. 1, right side), which fresco is aligned with the *tondo* now in the middle of the

ceiling as well as the central fresco on the opposite wall and should therefore be slightly to the right of the wall's physical centre. The figure of 1.8m is derived from 9 *braccia* or 5.3m (distance from historic centre at which area of Twelve perhaps began) minus 2½ *braccia* or 1.5m (margin of error for width of *residenza* and *porticciuola*) minus 2m (allowance for possibly different position of historic centre from present decorative centre). The figure of 8.4m comes from 9 *braccia* plus 2 *braccia* (margin of error) = 11 *braccia* or 6.4m plus 2.0m (allowance). The greatest likelihood perhaps is that the historic centre of the east wall was aligned with the centre of the ceiling, which in turn—if the ceiling was symmetrical—had to be aligned with the physical centre of the narrower west wall, the position of which has not changed appreciably. In that case the historic centre of the east wall is likely to have been almost exactly where its decorative centre is today.

55  See Vasari-Milanesi, IV, pp. 450–51; and n. 59.

56  Wilde (as in n. 15), p. 73; and Rubinstein, *Palazzo Vecchio*, p. 71. The great *ringhiera* in front of the Palace, on which numerous ceremonies took place and from which constitutional reforms were proposed to the people (it no longer exists), had three rows of (stone) benches and was about 2.5–2.8m high; ibid., p. 111.

57  See p. 9 at n. 21.

58  See the discussion beginning on p. 8 at n. 15.

59  One of these speaks of 775 [square?] *braccia* (452.6m or 264.3m$^2$) of boards for the floor (*palco*) and other parts of the *ringhiera*, and 454 *braccia* (265.1m) of *correnti* (small beams) out of which to make dentils and cornices for it; Operai di Palazzo, 6, fol. 62v (1496). Others tell of hundreds of balusters and several dozens of metres of *spalliere* (wainscotting);

e.g., 6, fols. 62v, 67v and 72r (1496 and 1497); and 8, fols. 136r-v, 137v, 140v, 141r and 141v (all 1500). But nowhere are we told what the *ringhiera* looked like or how many rows of benches or individual seats it had. We know only that its access stairs were made of stone (see n. 72) and that at least some of it had a stone parapet; 6, fol. 62v: 'braccia 54 (31.5m) di pietra abozata per il parapetto della ringhiera . . . conducte in sulla Sala . . .' ('54 *braccia* [31.5m] of blocked-out stone for the parapet of the *ringhiera* . . . brought into the Hall . . .').

60    See n. 64. It is likely that Vasari gives the correct height; see n. 72.

61    That is, in the case of the Sixteen, 16 x 0.63m (maximum amount of bench space probably occupied by each official) + 2.9m (maximum space taken up by 'little door' and sliver of wall on either side of it).

62    In Tratte, Uffici Intrinseci, bobina 6, a spool reproducing a volume listing public officials who served in the city, one counts 356 of them (including 34 notaries but not the foreign appointees) as of June 1505. To this astonishing number that of the consuls or captains of the 21 guilds (of whom there were at least four per guild) should almost certainly be added; cf. Deliberazioni, 121 (1519), fol. 119v (concerning an offering to be made at the Cathedral): 'cum . . . omnibus magistratibus civitatis Florentie, et specialiter et nominatim spectabili[bus] Sex Curie Mercantie una cum eorum Capitudinibus [*scil.: of the Guilds*] . . .' ('with . . . all the magistrates of the city of Florence, and especially and expressly the esteemed Six of the Court of the *Mercanzia* [Merchants' Court] together with their Captains [*scil.: of the Guilds*] . . .'); also 122 (1520), fol. 106v, etc. The members of the Council of the Eighty were considered magistrates as well; Deliberazioni, 130 (1528), fols. 79v, 86r, etc. (concerning *Consigli di Quarantia* or appeals boards):

'et alij de Magistratibus & numero Octuaginta . . .' ('and other of the Magistrates and members of the Eighty . . .'). As is clear from the text of any *provvisione*, the Eighty were considered part of the executive during meetings of the Major Council. The number of magistrates present may therefore have exceeded—in theory if not in practice—500 persons, requiring, one imagines, at least 450 *braccia* or 263m of bench space. The circumference of the Hall was just under 160m, of which at least 25m must have been occupied by doorways, the stairs to the *ringhiera*, the *residenza* of the *Signoria*, the altar, and so on.

63  See, for example, Wilde (as in n. 15), pp. 71, 75, etc.; and Rubinstein, *Palazzo Vecchio*, p. 41. The *aliette* (little wings) of the *residenza* of the *Signoria* in the Great Hall almost certainly imitated the projecting wings of the government's tribune in the Sala del Maggior Consiglio at Venice. For these *aliette* see Frey (as in n. 16), p. 121, nos. 70 and 77 (1498 and 1499); p.122, no. 84 (1499); and p. 123, nos. 95, 99 and 104 (all 1500). The Venetian hall is illustrated in fig. 14 of Rubinstein's book.

64  Tuscan choir stalls of the period are usually around 75cm wide. But in the Sala dell'Udienza, whereas the *Signori* were in *sederi* (seats almost certainly other than benches; see n. 50), the *Collegi* sat on benches: 'panche coperte di nocie, cornici, balauschj, tarsie et predelle . . . dove seghono e venerabilj Collegi' ('benches covered with walnut, cornices, balusters, intarsias and predellas . . . where the venerable Colleges [Colleagues?] sit'); Operai di Palazzo, 10, fol. 34r (1502). One also imagines that the *pancali* (buntings?) of cloth which set off the *Collegi* (see below) were more suited to benches (*panche*) than they would have been to individual seats. The great stone *ringhiera* in front of the Palace had benches (see n. 56). Vasari does say, to be sure, that the *ringhiera* of the Hall had 'sederi a uso di

teatro' ('seats of the kind used in theatres'); ed. Milanesi, IV, p. 450. There is little indication that the parts of the *ringhiera* occupied by the *Collegi* were different from those which accommodated the other magistrates. From an entry of 1512 it does appear, however, that the *Collegi* were set off by special decorations of cloth; Camera dell'Arme, 21, fol. 6v; and 40, fol. 21b: 'per rimendatura . . . d'una spalliera de' Chollegj della Sala Grande, c[i]oè un pa[n]chale' ('for the mending of . . . a *spalliera* of the Colleges [Colleagues?] of the Great Hall, that is, a *pancale*'). It is possible that the *Collegi* sat in single rows, whereas the other magistrates (except perhaps for the Ten of Liberty and Peace; see n. 97) sat in double rows.

65　The sum of 6.4m (maximum distance of seating area of Twelve from historic centre) and 3.8m (maximum width of this area, if we assume that the Twelve sat in two rows and that each of them required no more than 63cm of bench space) is 10.2m. If the Twelve sat in a single row and therefore occupied up to 7.6m, the space in which Leonardo began might have ended as far as 14.0m (6.4 + 7.6m) from the wall's historic centre. If the Twelve sat in stalls rather than on benches, the distances from the historic centre at which their section of the *ringhiera* ended might have been around 10.9m (6.4 + 4.5m), or 15.4m (6.4 + 9.0m) if they sat in a single row.

66　As the scene probably was somewhat less than 5m wide (see immediately below), it could have extended up to, say, 15.0m (10.2 + 4.8m) from the historic centre (15.7m if the Twelve sat in stalls)—or even 18.8m (14.0 + 4.8m) if they sat in a single row (20.2m if they sat in stalls). On the slight possibility that the standard was to have been displayed physically rather than painted, see p. 39 at n. 120.

67　See n. 4.

68  Frey (as in n. 16), p. 136, no. 244 (30 April 1513), where we read of 'braccia 43 d'asse di terzo d'albero' ('43 *braccia* of boards of a third [of a *braccio*] of poplar'). Some experts have construed that to mean that the scene had an area of (somewhat less than) 14 2/3 (43 ÷ 3) square *braccia* or 4.9m², others that its perimeter measured 43 *braccia* or 25.1m, giving the scene the equally improbable area of around 109 square *braccia* or 37.3m². It is remarkable how many key documents Frey overlooked. Equally remarkable is how many irrelevant documents he published.

69  Operai di Palazzo, 14, fol. 5r: 'Da Francesco di Capello e Compagni lengniaiuolj e soctoscrict[i] lengniamj, e qualj levò Rinierj Locti fino addì 22 di giennaro, disse per fare un'armadura jn Sala dela Guardia ala pictura fecie Leonardo da Vincj perché la non si guastassj, cioè: xxviiij asse d'albero dj terzo, le quale furono braccia 43— quadre; a ß4 [il] braccio [quadro] montano — — £8.12 —' ('From Francesco di Capello and Company, woodworkers, the hereinafterwritten wood, which was picked up by Rinieri Lotti on the 22nd day of January, he said . . . [*as in text*]; at 4 *soldi* a [square] *braccio* they amount to —— £8.12 —'). (This was a considerable sum.) The remodelling of the Hall into a barracks was not yet finished as of 31 December 1512, as a 'deliberation' of that date concerns 'habietes . . . que jn futurum habebuntur a dicta Opera [*scil.: of Santa Maria del Fiore*] pro conficiendis mansionibus Custodie Sale Nove' ('fir trees . . . that will be received in the future from the said *Opera* [*scil.: of Santa Maria del Fiore, that is, the Cathedral*] for making the living quarters of the Guard of the New Hall'); Deliberazioni, 114, fol. 141v. See also n. 15. That a Medicean government should have taken measures to protect an unfinished work presumably painted to glorify the Republic, says a great deal about how highly esteemed Leonardo's painting was.

70   If the boards were fashioned into a shallow box or crate, the area covered might have been around 12m². It is unlikely to have been less than that, for in that case two *quaderni* (at least 13.25m²) of paper, sufficient to make a usable surface of at least 11.7m², would have been enough to transfer the design for the scene to the wall, rather than the three that were actually bought. (We are assuming that the paper in question was used for the duplicate cartoon from which the painting evidently was made; see p. 44 at n. 139.) It also is possible that different (unrecorded) wood was used to make a framework; in that case the boards may have covered a painted surface of up to 14.5m². (We also are assuming that at least most of the scene was taken up by the figures and that there was very little—if any—surrounding ground or sky.)

71   *Il Codice Magliabechiano cl. XVII.17 contenente notizie sopra l'arte . . .*, ed. C. Frey, Berlin, 1892, p. 114: 'et dipoj . . . volse mettere [quello stucco] in opera nella Sala, dove giù basso il fuoco agiunse et seccholla, ma lassù alto, per la distantia grande, non vi aggiunse il calore, et colò' ('and afterwards he tried to apply [that *stucco*] in the Hall, where down low the fire reached it and dried it, but high up there, on account of the great distance, the heat did not get there, and it ran'). One has severe doubts about this statement: if the *stucco* 'high up there' really failed to dry properly whereas the rest did, why did Leonardo not simply remake it, rather than becoming 'indignant' and leaving, as the anonymous writer would have us believe? But something evidently did go wrong with at least some of Leonardo's specially prepared surface (perhaps only after many years; see n. 100), as Antonio Billi, Vasari and Paolo Giovio also speak of its being defective (see below). The anonymous writer believed that Leonardo had taken the idea for his preparation from the Roman natural historian Pliny (the Elder); ibid. Billi says that Leonardo worked with 'materia che non

serrava [seccava?]' ('material that did not take [dry?]'), and this because a supplier had cheated him with falsified linseed oil; *Il Libro di Antonio Billi esistente . . . nella Biblioteca Nazionale di Firenze*, ed. C. Frey, Berlin, 1892, p. 52. One has doubts about this statement also: Leonardo did not buy the linseed (and walnut) oil; the *Opera* of the Palace bought it for him, and it is hard to believe that any of the *Opera*'s suppliers, most of whom served it for decades, would have tried to cheat it over such a relatively small matter. Frey (as in n. 16), p. 132, no. 183 (1504); p. 134, nos. 211 and 215–17; and p. 135, nos. 232–33 and 236 (all 1505). See also Vasari-Milanesi, IV, p. 43; and Paolo Giovio, 'Leonardi Vinci vita', in *Scritti d'arte del Cinquecento*, ed. P. Barocchi, Milan and Naples, I, 1971, pp. 8–9. The copy dated 1553 is a drawing in the Uffizi; the date on it was recently detected by Maurizio Seracini.

72   Vasari-Milanesi, IV, p. 450. A record of February 1497 speaks of a piece of stone measuring 3 *braccia* for the [an] entrance (*uscio*) to the *ringhiera*; Operai di Palazzo, 6, fol. 67v. Access to the *ringhiera* was by means of stone steps; see below. Vasari says (IV, p. 451) that there were six of these steps per staircase. But from the same record it appears instead that each staircase had eight steps: 'ischagl[i]onj di pietre gentilj per la ringhiera della Sala £5 l'uno £40' ('steps of fine stone for the *ringhiera* of the Hall £5 apiece £40'). That Vasari is correct about the height of the *ringhiera* also seems likely in view of the fact that the windows on the west wall of the Hall appear to have started at a height of about 3 *braccia* or 1.75m (if we assume that the level of the floor is slightly [5cm] higher now because of repaving). Underneath the *Udienza* by Bandinelli and others (Fig. 1, middle) one can see where a new pavement was laid over a previous one (the original?). The floor of the Hall was repaved, perhaps for the last time, in 1882 with the pattern we see today or one very

much like it. At that time the previous flooring, which apparently had a similar pattern, was removed. Archivio Storico del Comune di Firenze, CF6278 (Contratti d'Accollo), fasc. 54.

73 The *spalliere* in the Sala dei Settanta, for example, were 2 *braccia* or 1.2m high; Operai di Palazzo, 2, fol. 9r (1481). There is a good deal of information on the *spalliere* of the Great Hall in Operai di Palazzo, 8, fols. 136r–141v, passim (1500). These *spalliere* were quite expensive and appear to have been one of the Hall's main attractions. See n. 81; and Frey (as in n. 16), p. 136, no. 240 (Landucci, *Diario* [under December 1512]).

74 The *residenza* with its backing, which culminated in an entablature, can hardly have been much lower than 8 *braccia* or 4.7m, which is the level at which the stone strips that support the frames containing Vasari's frescoes now rest. For the *Signori* sat higher than all others, and the other magistrates probably sat at a height of 3 *braccia* or 1.75m; see n. 72. A decree of 1420 prohibited the *Podestà*, Captain, and Executor (all very highly paid foreign officials) to sit on the same level as the *Signoria*; Deliberazioni, 34, fol. 69v. In the Sala dell'Udienza (Hall of the Audience) the *Collegi* were at the feet of the *Signori*; Rubinstein, *Palazzo Vecchio*, p. 112. Vasari, who correctly uses the terms, 'residenza' and 'ringhiera', twice says that the *residenza* was 'più eminente', that is, higher (than the *ringhiera*); see n. 9. In Venice the government's tribune was well over 4.7m high; see the illustration in Rubinstein, *Palazzo Vecchio*, fig. 14. For the use of the word 'quadro' in Leonardo's agreement with the *Signoria*, see Frey, p. 130, no. 175 (or Villata [as in n. 1], p. 166, no. 189). That some of this *quadro* was to have been over the *residenza* seems clear from the fact that the windows there were walled up just before Leonardo began to paint (see n. 46), as well as the strong probability that his *quadro* was to have been at least half the wall in length (n. 141).

75 See pp. 27–28 beginning at n. 84.

76 The frames containing the 'incrustations' rest at a height of 4.85m. They in turn are supported by stone 'listre' (strips) having a thickness of about 15cm. The frames and *listre* are documented in Scrittoio delle Fortezze e Fabbriche, Fabbriche Medicee (henceforth: Fabbriche Medicee), 4, fols. 33v and 48r (1564 and 1566); see n. 86.

77 Thermography 'sees'—in this case through a layer of plaster and possibly more—by plotting the variations in the heat that emanates from the different parts of the wall under special conditions. For other observations by Seracini, see p. 30 at n. 93. On the installation of the additional windows in the side walls, see p. 40 before n. 121. On the rediscovery of some of the former west windows, see Newton and Spencer (as in n. 10), pp. 48–50.

78 Supposing that it was Vasari who built the ledge would, on the other hand, explain why no remnants of the east wall's original features (such as the two *porticciuole* or 'little doors' that once flanked the *residenza* of the *Signoria* or the probable doors to the latrines [see n. 40]) came to light when the plaster was removed from beneath Vasari's frescoes there in 1978. Another reason for supposing that it was Vasari who built this ledge is that, if it had been part of the Hall's original construction and once been visible, the windows installed in the west wall about a year after it was built would have been partly above and partly below it and therefore looked quite awkward.

79 E. Borsook, *The Mural Painters of Tuscany*, 2nd edn, Oxford, 1980, p. 60.

80 The sum of 4.7m (the level of the now invisible setback or ledge) + 0.15m (the thickness of the 'listre' or stone strips that

rest on it) + 0.8m (the thickness of the huge frames that rest on the 'listre') is 5.65m. It also is possible that Leonardo's battle mural was to have begun only around the level established by the tops of the windows on the west wall, which Newton and Spencer (as in n. 10), p. 48, report to have been 6.4m or 11 *braccia*. This probably was the approximate level at which the battle mural on the west wall was to have begun, if any such mural was planned; see pp. 43 at n. 133; and esp. 51, paragraph following n. 168. If there was to have been a battle mural on the west wall, it evidently would have had to be the one by Michelangelo; see p. 41 at n. 125; p. 43 at n. 132; and p. 52, paragraph following n. 171.

81   The room's original height was either 19 or, more probably, 20 *braccia* (11.1 or 11.7m); see n. 7. The richly documented *cornicione* or cornice on which its wooden ceiling appeared to rest must have been at least one *braccio* (0.6m) high. It cost 42 *soldi* (2 *lire* and 2 *soldi*) per *braccio* (Frey [as in n. 16], p. 117, no. 28 [1496]) or twice as much as the benches with backs (Frey, p. 118, no. 39). Even so, it cost only one third as much as the pieces of wainscotting or *spalliere* behind the *ringhiera* (Operai di Palazzo, 8, fol. 140v, etc.), one sixth as much as the benches of the Doctors of Law and the Ten of Liberty and Peace (Frey, pp. 125–26, no. 127, where 'XX' should read 'XII'), or one seventh as much as the entablature of the *residenza* of the *Signoria* before gilding (see n. 50).

82   If it survives, the scene may now be entirely underneath Vasari's fresco of the *Battle of Marciano* (and therefore rest at a level of no less than 5.65m), as Vasari hardly would have run an enormous stone frame through or over it if he meant to avoid causing damage to it. Indeed, one of the reasons why Vasari adopted the decorative scheme that he did, with a nar-

row painting in the centre and wide ones to either side, may have been to save Leonardo's painting.

83  (Of the cartoon:) 'E [Lionardo] vi fece un gruppo [*Vasari has* groppo (*tangle*)] tanto terribile, e in così nuova maniera, che insino all'hora non s'era veduto cosa non che più bella, che a gran pezzo la pareggiasse' ('And Leonardo made a group there so awesome and in such a new style that until then nothing had been seen that was not just more beautiful but came a long way from equaling it'); *Orazione funerale di M. Benedetto Varchi fatta e recitata da lui pubblicamente nell'esequie di Michelagnolo Buonarroti in Firenze*, Florence, Giunti, 1564, p. 17.  Benvenuto Cellini (as in n. 5) says that the horses in Leonardo's cartoon were 'tanto divinamente fatti quanto imaginar si possa' ('as divinely done as can be imagined'), and that it was 'bellissimo e mirabile' ('most beautiful and amazing').  What Vasari says is extremely perplexing in view of the fact that it was he who either destroyed the painting or else built a counter wall or membrane in front of the surface on which it is painted.  Like Varchi and Cellini, both of whose source he is, Vasari greatly praises the cartoon, of which he at first speaks in the past tense (as do Varchi and Cellini), saying that it *was* thought to be most excellent and thus clearly implying that it no longer existed in his day (ed. Milanesi, IV, pp. 41–42).  But as he describes the *Capture of a Standard* section, which he clearly—and incorrectly—believes to have been all that Leonardo ever made (cf. also IV, p. 319), in the *present* tense and speaks of a *red* beret to be seen in it (!), it is clear that he never saw the cartoon and is really describing the painting.  Of the painting, however, Vasari says only that Leonardo abandoned it after a short time because the preparation (*incollato*) on which he was painting it began to run (IV, p. 43), leaving one with the impression that there never was anything of interest by Leonardo on the walls of the Hall.

Everything that Vasari says about the cartoon and painting is already present in his edition of 1550; see Vasari (as at the end of n. 9), IV, pp. 31–33. In other words, he added no new information about Leonardo's scene after he began working in the Hall around 1560, at which time the painting almost certainly still existed in an at least acceptable state; see nn. 101 and 102.

84 Fabbriche Medicee, 4, fol. 46v (1566): 2000 *scudi di moneta* are paid to a *muratore* (builder, contractor) 'per havere alzatto el tetto . . . braccia 12 a tutte sue ispese' ('for having raised the roof . . . 12 *braccia*, all expenses his'). See also n. 7.

85 Fabbriche Medicee, 5, fols. 9v: '14,405 mezzane roze ala campig[i]ana . . . per fare la 'nc[r]ostatura dela fac[i]ata di verso [*sic*] deto Salone di verso le scale [*scil., towards the west*] per dipignervi istorie, fato per ordine di G[i]org[i]o Vasarj . . .' ('14,405 *mezzane rozze alla campigiana* [rough *mezzane*, country style] . . . to make the incrustation on the wall of the said *Salone* [Great Hall] towards the stairs in order to paint stories [scil., narrative paintings] there, done on the orders of Giorgio Vasari'); 19r: [*to a builder*] 'per l'incostratura [*sic*] fatta nella fac[i]ata [*scil., the west wall*] del Salone di detto Palazo per dipigniervj le storie della guerra dj Pisa . . .' ('for the incrustation made on the wall of the *Salone* of the said Palace in order to paint the stories of the War of Pisa there . . .'); 22r: '3418 di mezane roze ca[m]pig[i]ane . . . per fare lo 'ncostrame[n]tto [*sic*] dele fac[i]ate di detto Salone dove van[n]o le storie' ('3418 *mezzane rozze campigiane* . . . to make the incrustation of the walls of the said *Salone* where the stories are going'); 25r: '14,310 di mezane roze al[l]a canpig[i]ana . . . per fare le 'ncostrature dele fac[i]ate per fare le storie' ('14,310 *mezzane rozze alla campigiana* . . . to make the incrustations of the walls to make the stories'); and 27r: '7110 mezane roze . . . per

fare 1° incostramento per 1ª istoria delle fac[i]ate del Salone' ('7110 *mezzane rozze* . . . to make an incrustation for a story on the walls of the *Salone*'). The *incrostature* on the west wall were made in 1566 and 1567 (fols. 9v and 19r) and those on the east wall between June 1569 and the end of 1570 (fols. 22r, 25r, and 27r). The one on the right or south side of the east wall was the last to be made; see Muccini (as in n. 7), p. 133. See also E. Allegri and A. Cecchi, *Palazzo Vecchio e i Medici*, Florence, 1980, pp. 261–63.

86   *Mezzane* are almost never used in this way. I owe the measurements of Vasari's frescoes, as well as numerous others, to Maurizio Seracini. On 14 October 1564, and again on 28 February 1566, payment was made for 174 2/5 *braccia* (101.8m) of *pietra serena* (a fine gray sandstone often used in and around Florence) as well as 60 *braccia* (35.0m) of *listre* with which the frames and the strips underneath them in the west and east walls respectively would be or had already been made; Fabbriche Medicee, 4, fols. 33v and 48r. The frames apparently were installed in time for the splendid wedding of Crown Duke Francesco I de' Medici to Joan of Austria in December 1565; see Vasari-Milanesi, VIII, p. 572. The 'incrustations' were made only later; see n. 85. For the number of *mezzane* supplied, see ibid.

87   These computations assume 1cm of mortar between any two adjacent *mezzane* and 1cm of plaster on the outer surface of the 'incrustations'. In sixteenth-century Florentine walls one usually finds slightly more.

88   The number 39,243 may, however, not represent the full amount purchased, as in the records there is a break between October 1568 and July 1570.

89   In addition to the possibility that there were more *mezzane* than the ones about which we are informed (see the preceding

note), there is evidence that some stones were used along with the *mezzane*; see n. 91. There thus may have been more *mezzane* than were needed for six 'incrustations' having a uniform thickness of about 15.6cm, and so it is possible that some of the incrustations are thicker than 15.6cm in places. In any case the penetrating radar scan performed on it in 2002 established that the incrustation bearing Vasari's *Battle of Marciano*, which measures 7.5 x 12.4m and is probably the fresco that covers the piece of wall once or still partly filled by Leonardo's *Capture of a Standard*, is uniformly 15.6cm thick; see the following note.

90  M. Pieraccini, D. Mecatti, G. Luzi, M. Seracini, G. Pinelli, and C. Atzeni, 'Non-Contact Intrawall Penetrating Radar for Heritage Survey: The Search of the "Battle of Anghiari" by Leonardo da Vinci', *NDT&E International* (www.sciencedirect.com), XXXVIII, 2005, pp. 151–57.

91  Maurizio Seracini has found evidence that Vasari's 'incrustations' contain a few courses of stone as well as *mezzane*. Seracini has been able to 'see' the courses of stone by means of thermography. He is the founder of Editech, a world leader in art diagnostics, and will be conducting the forthcoming search for the painting.

92  That Vasari made the 'incrustations' so he could have surfaces ideal for painting frescoes is clear from the wording of the records cited in n. 85. The one flaw in these otherwise excellent surfaces is the large crack in the right-hand part of the *Battle of Marciano*, in a spot somewhat to the right of where Leonardo's *Capture of a Standard* probably was or is. This crack is so bad that it has caused the stone frame to separate. The crack may be due to a spiral staircase in the wall behind it.

93  These photographs are conserved in the Fototeca of the Soprintendenza per i Beni Artistici e Storici per le Provincie di Firenze,

Pistoia e Prato. *Intonaco* is the outer layer of fine plaster with which walls or ceilings in Italy are usually surfaced.

94 Seracini claims that when one is at the top of this part of the wall, one can feel a draught between its front and rear layers. On the last 'incrustation' see n. 85.

95 See p. 24 at n. 78.

96 The two *porticciuole* were separated by the *residenza* (probably 12 *braccia* or 7.0m) and, one imagines, a small amount of space on either side of it; see p. 16 at n. 50. These *porticciuole* did not come to light when the plaster was removed from all of the east wall beneath Vasari's frescoes in 1978. The large modern doorway goes from 2.8 to 5.1m to the right or south of the wall's present decorative centre (Fig. 1, extreme right). In the corresponding position to the left or north of this centre, as thermography shows, the wall has been rebuilt. Still it is possible, if Vasari added a new layer of masonry to this part of the wall (see p. 29 at n. 78), that remnants of the left or north *porticciuola* still exist underneath this layer and can someday be detected.

97 See p. 40 before n. 121; and nn. 14 and 46. Two documents of November 1513 tell of 'libbre xxxj½ di finestra ferata messa nela Sala Grande per la Guardia dove stavano già e X [Dieci]' ('31½ pounds of barred window put in the Great Hall for the Guard where the Ten used to be'); and of 'libbre 33 d'una finestra ferata di 6 ferrj messa nela Sala per la Guardia' ('33 pounds of a barred window of 6 iron bars put in the Hall for the Guard')—presumably for the twin of the window just described; Operai di Palazzo, 14, fol. 16v (both previously uncited). These windows, which cannot have been very large, as 5½-lb. (1.9-kg) iron bars cannot have been very long, may well have been at least part of the probably two that had been over the *residenza* or tribune of the *Signoria* from 1496 until the

end of 1504. The very powerful Ten (of Liberty and Peace or of *Balìa* [Power, Authority]), that is, the War Commissioners, had sat directly in front of the *Signoria*, along with the Doctors of Law. (In 1508 there had been at least 13 such Doctors, one of whom was the noted historian Francesco Guicciardini; Deliberazioni, 110, fol. 44r-v.) Frey (as in n. 16), p. 126, no. 130 (1502): 'dove seghono e Doctorj e X nella Sala Grande dinanzi alla Signoria' ('where the Doctors and Ten sit in the Great Hall in front of the *Signoria*'); and also p. 125, no. 127 (1502): 'ante altare Verginis et residentia Dominorum ubi resident Doctores et X Balìe' ('in front of the Altar of the Virgin and the *residenza* of the *Signori*, where the Doctors and the Ten of *Balìa* reside'). See Fig. 5. In 1505 the Ten had been served by a *provveditore* (manager, accountant), a *sottoprovveditore* (assistant manager or accountant), and at least five secretaries, one of whom was the famous political theorist and historian Niccolò Machiavelli (Dieci di Balìa, Deliberazioni, Condotte e Stanziamenti, 52, fols. 84$^r$ and 122v). At least some of these persons had no doubt sat with them in the Hall. In front of the *Signoria* there had also been the desk or table (*desco*) of the *banditori* or criers (Operai di Palazzo, 10, fols. 64v–65$^r$ [1504]) and a table or counter (*banco*) with an electoral urn of copper or brass containing 1,000 'ballots' of gilded or silvered copper (Provvisioni, 187 [bobina 370], fols. 36v–38r [1496]; both previously uncited).

98  The windows, if they were two, probably were about 6–8m apart, as we hear once of their being over the *residenza* of the *Signoria*, which probably was 7.0m wide, and once of one of them's being over 'the head of' the Twelve Good Men. See n. 14. The exact position of the piece of arch, which is visible in a photograph taken from behind the wall in the 1970s, is unknown.

99 If there in fact is a space between the original wall and Vasari's 'incrustation', fibre-optical endoscopy might be an effective means for detecting the painting.  However, endoscopy may not work if there is little or no space or if the painting is covered with whitewash or plaster.  In that case needle samples may need to be taken or a search device invented (one such device is already being worked on) that can sense the presence of pigments even through 15.6cm of terracotta and plaster without the need for drilling.  For the probable area of the painting, see p. 20.  Two hundred and four Florentine pounds (69.2kg) of linseed oil and 89 lbs 6 oz. (30.3kg) of pitch were bought, evidently for Leonardo's special surface, in March or April 1505; Frey (as in n. 16), p. 134, nos. 215 and 217.  If we may assume that 10 lbs (3.3kg) of oil were enough to produce at least 10 litres—that is, the amount needed to cover a square metre of wall to a depth of 1cm—of the special preparation, and that 4.4 lbs (1.5kg) of pitch were enough to seal at least one square metre of wall surface, we arrive at an area of at least 20.4m$^2$ and probably a good deal more.

100 Billi (as in n. 71); *Codice Magliabechiano* (as in n. 71), p. 114; and Vasari-Milanesi, IV, p. 43.  See also Giovio (1556; as in n. 71).  Writing in 1510, Francesco Albertini simply lists the painting without saying anything about its condition; *Memoriale di molte statue et Picture sono nella inclyta Ciptà di Florentia . . .* (ed. C. and G. Milanesi and C. Guasti, Florence, 1863, fol. a6r): 'li cavalli di Leonardo Vinci' ('the horses of Leonardo Vinci').

101 For example, the warrior visible at the lower left of the 'Doria' copy (Fig. 2), which is likely to be the earliest of the painted copies, is not mentioned by Vasari (who, although he says he is describing the cartoon, must really be describing the painting; see n. 83) and is not seen in the 'Uffizi' copy either (Fig. 3). (This warrior is seen, however, in a drawing in the Uffizi on

which Seracini has discovered the date of 1553, which year is after the one in which Vasari wrote his description.) According to Seracini, carbon-14 tests show that the 'Uffizi' copy is a work of the seventeenth century or later. If so, it evidently was copied from some other (lost) work made before the end of 1570, when Vasari built the 'incrustation' in front of where Leonardo's painting probably was or is (see n. 85).

102 E salito le scale della Sala Grande, diligentemente date una vista a un gruppo di cavalli, e d'uomini (un pezzo di battaglia di Lionardo da Vinci) che vi parrà una cosa miracolosa' ('And having climbed the stairs of the Great Hall, diligently take a look at a group of horses and men [a battle piece by Leonardo da Vinci], which will strike you as a miraculous thing'); printed in G. Bottari, *Raccolta di lettere sulla pittura, scultura ed architettura*, Rome, 1759, III, p. 234. The first edition of Vasari's *Lives* was printed in 1550; the manuscript must have been completed at least a year before then.

103 The motifs that Vasari evidently borrowed are the two men on the ground, one of whom is about to stab the other in the mouth, in the *Battle of Marciano*, which fresco most likely is over the place where Leonardo's *Capture* was or is; and the horsemen fighting in the center of the *Rout of San Vincenzo*, which most likely faces it. Completed towards the end of 1497, the *Last Supper*, according to Antonio de Beatis, already was 'beginning to be spoiled' around 1517–18; Villata (as in n. 1), p. 264, no. 314.

104 Frey (as in n. 16), pp. 130–31, no. 175 (or Villata, pp. 166–68, no. 189); and J. Wilde, 'Michelangelo and Leonardo', *Burlington Magazine*, XCV, 1953, p. 70 (Wilde says that the cartoon was 'far from finished'); see also n. 138. Leonardo's agreement was with not the Gonfalonier of Justice, Piero Soderini, who

could take no official action by himself, but the whole *Signoria*. It was unusual for the *Signori* to deal with artists directly. In August 1528, during the Last Republic, they would also deal directly with Michelangelo, when they would assign to him the block of marble that ultimately would become the statue of *Hercules and Cacus* by Baccio Bandinelli just to the right of the main door of Palazzo Vecchio; Deliberazioni, 130, fols. 155v–156r.

105 C. Pedretti, *Leonardo inedito: Tre saggi*, Florence, 1968, p. 54: 'Addì 6 dj g[i]ugno 1505, in venerdì, al tocho delle 13 ore [*around 8:40AM*], comj[n]c[i]aj a colorire in Palazo, nel qual punto del posare il pennelo si guastò il tempo, e ssonò a bancho richiedendo li òmjnj a rag[i]one; il cartone si stracc[i]ò, l'acqua si versò, e rupesi il vaso dell'acqua che ssi portava; e subito si guastò il tempo, e ppiovè insino a sera acqua grandjssima, e stette il tempo come notte' ('On the 6th day of June 1505, on Friday, at the stroke of 13 hours, I began to paint in the Palace, at which point of laying my brush the weather broke, and it rang to be seated (?), summoning the men to their deliberations; the cartoon tore, the water spilled, and the jug for the water we were carrying broke; and suddenly the weather broke, and it rained a very heavy rain until evening, and the weather [time?] was like night'). 6 June 1505 in fact was a Friday; cf. Cerretani (as in n. 1), pp. 104 and 110.

106 See Pedretti, pp. 53–55. The bell that interrupted Leonardo's work appears to have been the same great bell that summoned the councilmen to Council; see n. 20. During Soderini's gonfaloniership summer meetings of the Council were usually on Thursday mornings and winter meetings on Sunday afternoons; however, the Council might meet at other times as well. The summer meetings might begin anytime between 11 and 14 hours (after sunset); the bell started ringing two hours ear-

lier. Provvisioni, 192 (bobina 374), fols. 21r–22v (1501): 'La Signoria facci sonare la campana a distesa una hora continua, come al presente si fa; et passata detta hora, subito cominci a fare rintochare, et duri tale rintocho un'altra hora continua, dando alla fine almeno cinquanta tochi con prestezza; et mentre che così rintocherà, la Signoria si truovi in sulla Sala, et al fine di detto rintocho facci serrare le porte di detta Sala; et non s'aprino di poi ad alchuno del Consiglio excepto che a' Collegi'. ('The *Signoria* shall have the bell sounded at full peal for an hour continuously, as is done at present; and when the said hour is past, it shall begin to have it toll, and the said tolling shall last another hour continuously, at the end giving fifty strokes rapidly; and while it tolls thus the *Signoria* shall betake itself to the Hall, and at the end of the said tolling it shall have the doors of the Hall closed; and they shall not thereafter be opened for anyone of the Council except for the *Collegi*'.) See also Rubinstein, 'Primi anni' (as in n. 2), p. 182. It seems odd indeed that Leonardo should have begun to paint just as a bad storm was about to begin and the councilmen were beginning to assemble, even if he still had two hours in which to finish up after the bell had started to ring. Perhaps the Council meeting caught him by surprise, as the day was not a Thursday.

107 One probable reason why many experts believe that Leonardo was actually painting by the end of April 1505 is that a number of entries in the payment records of the *Operai di Palazzo* (Works Commissioners of the Palace) that really belong under 30 June of that year are erroneously published by Frey (as in n. 16) under 30 April (pp. 134–35, nos. 222–29). The error is perpetuated by Villata (as in n. 1), pp. 184–85, no. 218. The Raffaello di Antonio *dipintore* (the painter) who assisted Leonardo and in fact was paid in March or April, was paid for his *opere* (days worked) in *lire* at the rate of a mason. The Ferrando Spagnolo who also assisted Leonardo but really was

first paid only in May or June, was paid a monthly salary in florins at the rate of a master painter. He received payment for two months (probably June and July) and had a helper who ground his colors. Frey, p. 134, nos. 220 and 223; and p. 135, no. 230. For a while Leonardo possibly refused to work. In one of his notebooks we read: 'Il Gonfalonjeri cancelli il libro, e 'l Sere mi facci 1ª scritta de' denari ricevuti, e po[i] io murerò liberamente' ('Let the Gonfalonier cancel the book, and let the notary make me a record of the money received, and then I shall build freely'). *Il Codice Atlantico di Leonardo da Vinci nella Biblioteca Ambrosiana di Milano*, Milan, 1894-1904, I, p. CCXXIX (fol.77rb).

108   On 2 July the janitor of the Hall received a raise of 35 *soldi* a month (almost 60 percent) 'per avere più faticha che prima' ('for having more work than before'); Camera dell'Arme, 15, fol. 20r. Some of the extra work was no doubt due to the presence in the Hall of Leonardo and his scaffolding (which was on wheels; Frey, p. 133, no. 206 [January-February 1505]). On 6 July Leonardo granted power of attorney to another party, whose name alas is illegible, for some unspecified reason; Notarile Antecosimiano, 16277 (Ser Antonio Parenti, 1505–7), fol. 30r-v (previously uncited). One imagines that he expected to be either going away or else extremely busy soon after that date.

109   See nn. 1 and 111. In his exposition Cerretani places Leonardo's beginning to paint between 9 and 14 October, but it is most unlikely that he really thinks that Leonardo began at that time; see text immediately following.

110   Operai di Palazzo, 10, fol. 79r: '1060 matonj a sej facce per l'andito che va nella Sala Nuova' ('1060 six-sided bricks for the hallway that goes to the New Hall'). Nine hundred and

fifty *quadroni* (square bricks or terracottas) had already been
supplied for the flooring of the entranceway by 31 December
1504; fol. 71v.

111 Cerretani (as in n. 1), p. 111. Cerretani says here that the
flags were 13 and that the helmet of the defeated Bartolomeo
d'Alviano—as well as pennants, a bear, and a wolf—was displayed in the Hall along with them.

112 Neri di Gino Capponi, *Commentari*, in *Rerum Italicorum
scriptores*, ed. L. A. Muratori, XVIII, Milan, 1731, col. 1195:
'Il Capitano nostro corse dall'altro lato con circa 400 cavalli in
battaglia, andò ad assaltare lo Stendardo inimico, e presolo, e
furono rotti . . .' ('Our Captain raced from the other side with
around 400 horse in battalion, went to assault the enemy Standard, and took it, and they were routed . . .'). The assault is also
mentioned in the *Trophaeum Anglaricum* by Leonardo Dati,
Florence, Biblioteca Riccardiana, MS 1207, fols. 47v–58r. It
is most unlikely that two Florentine soldiers simply wrested
the standard away from two of their armed adversaries, as we
see in Leonardo's scene. In a *provvisione* (law) passed by the
Councils on 9 and 11 July 1440, we read about the enemy and
the flags: 'hostes iusto prelio partim fugati, partim cum sig-
nis militaribus capti' ('the enemy after the battle having partly
fled, [and] partly been captured with their military insignia');
Provvisioni, 131 (bobina 256), fol. 126r. Surely the simplest
way to capture a flag is to take prisoner or slay those who are
carrying it or else cause them to throw it away and flee. Such
actions, however, are not easy to depict if one's main purpose
is to show that a flag was taken rather than just the capture,
slaying, or putting to flight of one or more soldiers. What we
would have seen (and hope to see again) in Leonardo's painting thus was (is) not what actually happened but something
the artist invented for the sake of artistic effect—just like the

costumes he depicted.  See also A. Cecchi, 'Niccolò Machia-velli e Marcello Virgilio Adriani.  Sul programma e l'assetto compositivo delle "Battaglie" di Leonardo e Michelangelo per la Sala del Maggior Consiglio in Palazzo Vecchio', *Prospettiva*, LXXXIII-IV, 1996, pp. 103–4 and passim.

113  As we see in one of his three battle drawings in the Accademia at Venice (no. 216).  On Leonardo's studies for his battle mural see *Leonardo da Vinci, Master Draftsman*, ed. C. Bambach, cat. exh. New York, Metropolitan Museum, 2003, pp. 477–88, 494–98 and 500–8; further references there.

114  A drawing for this scene, often called the *Cavalcade*, is pre-served at Windsor Castle (no. 12339r).  As a number of other artists, including Raphael, clearly knew the scene, it is evident that it once formed part of Leonardo's cartoon.  The drawing ends in a straight line on its right-hand side, quite possibly indicating the end of the mural.  For the note see J. P. Richter, *The Notebooks of Leonardo da Vinci*, New York, 1970, I, p. 303.

115  See text following.  In Leonardo's agreement with the *Signoria*, the mural is called a 'quadro' ('rectangular panel', 'painting') and a 'pictura' ('picture'), which words lead one to visualise it as a single picture rather than a sequence of clearly separate scenes; Frey (as in n. 16), p. 130, no. 175 (or Villata [as in n. 1], p. 166, no. 189).  The action also goes from right to left in a *cassone* or wedding chest panel, probably from the late fifteenth century, depicting the Battle of Anghiari and now at Dublin, in which we apparently see both of the standards cap-tured at Anghiari at the right (and elsewhere); Cecchi (as in n. 112), p. 104; on the two standards see n. 119.

116  Cerretani (as in n. 1), p. 110: 'Et stimossi questa rotta essere suta magg[i]ore che cosa da cento anni im qua et anche 200 . . .'

('And this rout was held to have been greater than anything in the last hundred years and even 200 . . .'). On Michelangelo's beginning at the start, see p. 46 at n. 149. On the elimination of the windows, see p. 14 at n. 46. On Leonardo's possibly not having begun over the *Signoria* because his scaffolding could not yet be positioned over their *residenza*, see n. 167.

117 For example, a drawing in the Accademia at Venice (no. 215) clearly appears to be a study leading to the scene. Another of the three battle drawings at Venice and at least one of those at Windsor also may be studies for it.

118 One of our earliest sources reports that the major part of Leonardo's cartoon was left with other of Leonardo's belongings at the Florentine hospital of Santa Maria Nuova. This major part was the part that did *not* represent the *Capture of a Standard*, which (minor) part instead was in the Great Hall; *Codice Magliabechiano* (as in n. 71), p. 111. Clearly, then, Leonardo had already prepared a good deal—but probably not all—of his material by the time he started painting. And surely he had already worked out the placement of the several scenes that were ready or almost ready to be painted. He certainly had, if, as appears very likely, his cartoon originated as a single 'quadro' or 'pictura' having a hem around it, rather than in several pieces; see nn. 115 and 139.

119 An inventory of 1458 shows that the two standards were in the Palace in the Room of the Gonfalonier as of that year. See N. Rubinstein, 'Machiavelli and the Mural Decoration of the Hall of the Great Council of Florence', in *Musagetes: Festschrift für Wolfram Prinz*, ed. R. G. Kecks, Berlin, 1991, p. 282. The standards were a white one with a leopard representing the *condottiere* Niccolò Piccinino and a red one with the device of the Duke of Milan (ibid.). We do not know which of the

two—if either—Leonardo planned to depict. The standards are also mentioned by the merchant and chronicler Benedetto Dei (*La cronica dall'anno 1400 all'anno 1500*, ed. R. Banducci, Florence, 1984, p. 56 [fol. 16r]), who reports that they (first) were hung upside down in the Cathedral, 'e llì stanno a perpetua memoria e ffama' ('and they are there for perpetual memory and fame').

120 This possible other scene might have been the so-called *Cavalcade* (Fig. 7), showing a reserve corps about to go into action (see p. 37 at n. 113). The wall's southern end is where the representation of the whole battle probably was to have begun (ibid.). The theory just proposed could explain why the cartoon tore, the water spilled, and the water jug broke when the storm occurred on 6 June 1505, as the southern end of the wall was close to what may then have been the Hall's three largest windows; in any case the window in the middle of the south wall almost certainly was by far the largest in the room; see nn. 105 and 128. My thanks to Maurizio Seracini for pointing out this possibility to me.

121 Vasari-Milanesi, IV, p. 450.

122 That there in fact were three windows in each of the end walls is confirmed by visual evidence on the outside of the north wall as well as by three entries in Operai di Palazzo, 10: '6 sportelli alle finestre di testa . . . verso santo Piero Scaragio' (6 *sportelli* [hinged frames] for the windows at the end . . . towards San Piero Scheraggio [*a church now built into the northern end of the Uffizi*]'); 'per inpannare 12 sportegli alla Sala del Consigl[i]o Magiore' ('to pane with cloth 12 *sportelli* in the Hall of the Major Council'); both fol. 59v; and 'per i 12 sportegli della Sala del Consigl[i]o' ('for the 12 *sportelli* of the Hall of the Council'); fol. 60r (all 1504). (Last two

entries previously uncited. Italian windows almost always have two *sportelli*.) The two windows in the middle of the east wall were no doubt the ones over the *residenza* or tribune of the *Signoria* or over 'the head of' the *Collegi* (see nn. 14 and 35); the four in the west wall must have been the four mentioned in a document of 1504 (see n. 38). As a rule the windows were *impannate*, filled with cloth treated with wax. But one of them was at least partly of glass and had a coat of arms; Operai di Palazzo, 10, fol. 72v (1504): 'per rimectitura di 21 ochio [*sic*] di vetro messi di suo a più finestre, cioè [*in three other places*] et in Sala Grande et per una arme messa alla finestra della Sala Grande' ('for the replacement of 21 *occhi* [round pieces] of glass placed on his own in several windows, that is, [*in three other places*] and in the Great Hall, and for a coat of arms placed in the window of the Great Hall'; previously uncited). Five windows were installed in the Hall in May 1532. At least five doors existed there as of that month. Operai di Palazzo, 15, fol. 25v.

123 Vasari-Milanesi, IV, p. 451.

124 Ibid., IV, p. 41; and VII, p. 159. Vasari is followed by Varchi (as in n. 83). In view of the way he redecorated the Hall (after having consulted with Michelangelo), as well as what he says on IV, p. 451 ('come volleno i cittadini con animo d'ornarla [scil., la Sala], col tempo, di pitture e metter il palco d'oro' ['as the citizens had it in mind to decorate it (scil., the Hall), in time, with paintings and to gild the ceiling']), it seems clear that the *altra facciata* Vasari is talking about is the wall across from the one on which Leonardo was about to start working. He says that the Gonfalonier gave Michelangelo *the* other wall, not *an*other wall or part of a wall (see also n. 127). The question, then, is not which wall or piece of wall Vasari is speaking about, but whether he is correctly informed about

plans that had been made long before he was born and for the most part were never carried out. Cerretani also implies that the whole room was to have been painted. In his words Leonardo 'began to paint the Hall of the Council'. See n. 1. On the size of the cartoon according to Vasari, ed. Milanesi, VII, p. 160.

125 *Il Carteggio di Michelangelo*, ed. G. Poggi, reed. P. Barocchi and R. Ristori, Florence, III, 1973, p. 7: 'io avevo tolto a fare la metà della Sala del Consiglio di Firenze, cioè a dipigniere, che n'avevo tre mila ducati'. The letter was written in 1523, long after the fact, and the statements Michelangelo makes in it are often untruthful. It is most unlikely that the Florentine Republic expected to pay Michelangelo anything even remotely approaching 3000 florins, which famous gold coins the artist, like many others at the time, always refers to as 'ducats'. The price that Michelangelo really was to have received would doubtless have been determined through arbitration at the time of the work's completion, just like the price of Leonardo's mural (and that of Michelangelo's own *David*); cf. Leonardo's agreement with the *Signoria* (Frey [as in n. 16], pp. 130–31, no. 175; or Villata [as in n. 1], pp. 166–68, no. 189). But Michelangelo's assertion that he was to have received 3000 'ducats' at least gives us some sense of the magnitude of his projected mural in the artist's memory. Although obviously not so large, he nevertheless evidently considered it to be comparable to the frescoes of the Sistine Ceiling, for the price of which he also gives 3000 ducats (which in this case they really were).

126 Wilde (as in n. 15). The eighteenth-century Vatican librarian Giovanni Bottari clearly believed that the two works were to have been across from each other, even if he was somewhat confused: 'Questo è il celebre cartone di Lionardo da Vinci

non terminato, dirimpetto al quale ne fece un altro Michelagnolo, e ambedue son periti' ('This is the celebrated unfinished cartoon of Leonardo da Vinci, across from which Michelangelo made another one, and both have perished'). Bottari (as in n. 102), III, p. 234, n. 3. One scholar who did not believe that the two murals were to have been on opposite walls was Wilhelm Köhler ('Michelangelos Schlachtkarton', *Kunstgeschichtliches Jahrbuch der k. k. Zentral-Kommission . . . [Wiener Jahrbuch für Kunstgeschichte]*, I, 1907, esp. p. 170). On the size of the murals see preceding note; and pp. 41–52 beginning at n. 124. On what Michelangelo earned for his work on the Sistine Ceiling, see R. Hatfield, *The Wealth of Michelangelo*, Rome, 2002, pp. 123–25.

127 Wilde, esp. pl. 18 (also illustrated in H. Hibbard, *Michelangelo*, New York, 1974 [1979], p. 78). Wilde surely would not have arrived at these conclusions if he had known about the evidence presented here or realised how much paper Leonardo used (see p. 44 at n. 137). He says (p. 80) that Michelangelo's assertion that he had undertaken to paint 'half the Hall' and Vasari's that Piero Soderini had given Michelangelo 'the other wall' (*l'altra facciata*) must both be taken metaphorically; see nn. 124 and 125. I am unable to think of any clear instance in Vasari's *Lives* in which the word 'facciata' means part of the surface of a wall rather than its entire surface, as Wilde would have us believe (or any clear instance in Michelangelo's letters in which 'half' means less than one sixth!). In all other cases in which Vasari uses 'facciata' in connection with the Hall (ed. Milanesi, IV, pp. 450, 452 and 453; VI, pp. 171, 172 and 174; and VII, p. 702), the word denotes an entire surface. Wilde believes (p. 81) that Leonardo's *Capture* would have occupied somewhat more than one seventh of his battle mural and Michelangelo's *Bathing Soldiers* about one fifth of his.

128  The windows in the west wall were 4.5m (4.7m or 8 *braccia*?) tall and 2.3m or 4 *braccia* wide. The windows in the east wall, when they existed, can hardly have been much taller; see n. 46. The arched window still visible, together with most of the round window over it, from the outside in the middle of the north wall, is the same size as the west windows once were. So probably were the other two windows in the north wall, a piece of one of which is still visible from the outside. But one of the documents mentions 'una finestra grande' ('a large window'), implying that there were windows of different sizes in the Hall and that there were at least two of the large kind; Operai di Palazzo, 8, fol. 98v (1497; previously uncited). These 'large windows', if they indeed were larger than the windows in the west and north walls, can only have been the ones in the south wall. One of these (no doubt the one in the middle) clearly was much larger than all the rest, as two of the surviving records speak of 'la finestra grande (del Consigl[i]o)' ('the great window [of the Council]'), the curtain of which contained 96 *braccia* or 56.1m of blue cloth; fol. 99r (1497; both documents previously uncited). A curtain for one of the west or north windows would have required, one imagines, at most 48 *braccia* or 28.0m of cloth—that is, 6 lengths of 8 *braccia* or 4.7m each—or slightly more. The area of each of the west windows was about 9.8m², as is the area of the window still fully visible on the north. That of the 'great window' was, by analogy with the altarpiece, which measures 4.44 x 3.04m (12.5m²) and for the curtain of which six lengths of 8 *braccia* (4.7m) or 28.0m of cloth were used (Camera dell'Arme, 31 [1529], fol. 43r), about 25.0m² or two and a half times as great. The height of the 'great window' possibly was or approached 12 *braccia* or 7.0m (8 lengths of 12*br* = 96*br*; 8 x 7.0m = 56.0m); if so, its width perhaps was around 6½ *braccia* or 3.8m (or else 6 *braccia* or 3.5m, that is, half its height, in which case the 'great window's' area would have been 23.2m²).

129   There probably were at least four *occhi*, one of which was much larger than the others.  In Operai di Palazzo, 10, on fol. 74ᵛ (1505), we read of '3 ochi alla Sala del Consigl[i]o' ('3 *occhi* in the Hall of the Council').  These three oculi or round windows must have been very small, as 5½ *braccia* (about 3.2m) of cloth were enough to fill both them and two *sportelli* (hinged window frames, shutters, doors in furniture, etc.) in the room of the Gonfalonier's wife; fol. 75r.  But another oculus, which evidently was the only one of its kind (and must therefore be the one in the middle of the north wall part of which can still be seen from outside and which has a diametre of 2.0m), was much larger, as it took 7 *braccia* or 4.1m of cloth to fill it; Operai di Palazzo, 8, fol. 105r (1498): 'braccia vij di panno lino di Lione per l'ochio della Sala Grande' ('7 *braccia* of linen of Lyons for the *occhio* of the Great Hall').  The seven *braccia* of linen cost 3 *lire* and 17 *soldi*, that is, 11 *soldi* per *braccio*.  Also 10, fol. 40r (1502): 'per inpannare più finestre alla Sala Nuova, cioè l'ochio grande et uno picholo' ('to pane with cloth some windows in the New Hall, that is, the large *occhio* and a small one').  (All four documents previously uncited.)  One can still see two *occhi* of much different sizes when viewing the outside of the north wall of the Hall today.

130   The windows on the west wall appear to have been at a height of only 3 *braccia* or 1.75m (they are now at 1.7m), that is, the probable level of the floor of the *ringhiera* or magistrates' gallery that ran around the Hall.  Those on the north wall, certainly one and probably all three of which were the same size as those on the west wall (see n. 128), appear to have been at 5 *braccia* or 2.9m (they are now at 2.8m)—possibly the level to which the *spalliere* or wainscotting behind the *ringhiera* came.  Those on the east wall must have been at a height of at least 8 *braccia* or 4.7m in order to have been 'over the *residenza* of the *Signoria*'.  See pp. 22–23 beginning at n. 73; and n. 46.

We know nothing about where the windows of the south wall were positioned; its 'great window' obviously cannot have been placed very high.

131 See the diagram in Newton and Spencer (as in n. 10), p. 50. On the level of the floor of the *ringhiera*, see p. 22 at n. 72. For evidence that one of the three windows on the south wall was of a much different size and that the other two may have been different also, see n. 128. The altarpiece, which is 4.44m tall (about the reported height of the north and west windows), was begun only in 1510. But the frame for it was already in place when Leonardo and Michelangelo were working or preparing to work in the Hall. This frame must have come to around the level established by the tops of the west windows, which Newton and Spencer, p. 48, give as 6.4m (11 *braccia*). Now, a window 4.5m tall positioned at a level of 1.7m ought to reach a height of 6.2 and not 6.4m, as Newton and Spencer report. I am unable to ascertain where the error lies. Perhaps the real height of these windows was 4.7m or 8 *braccia*.

132 See n. 46. For the probable height of the *residenza* or tribune of the *Signoria*, over which the east windows were positioned, see pp. 22–23 after n. 73. During the winter of 1504–5 a good deal of other construction was underway in the Hall; Operai di Palazzo, 10, fols. 71r, 71v, 72r, 74r and 74v. Some of this concerned the 'maghazino' or store room in or next to the *Segreto*; see p. 10 at n. 30. There also was work on an archway with a column in its middle somewhere in the Hall.

133 Seracini believes that there may have been five windows on the west wall rather than four. The Hall of the Major Council in Venice, which clearly was the main model for the one in Florence, had paintings on both of its side walls (which contain windows) as well as at least one of its end walls.

134 Operai di Palazzo, 10, fol. 73r (November-December 1504): 'un paio di capre a Michelagnolo di braccia 4 alte e lunghe 5 per dipignere el cartone . . .' ('a pair of trestles 4 *braccia* high and 5 long for Michelangelo to paint the cartoon . . .'). The cost of these trestles was one of the least important items in a carpenter's bill for two months amounting to 173 *lire* and 7 *soldi*. (Most of this price was for two *deschi* [desks, tables] with four *armarii* [cabinets?].) An additional one *lira* and 16 *soldi* were spent for the sawing of two old beams out of which the trestles and platform (*palco*) were made; Frey (as in n. 16), p. 133, no. 199 (where 'la capra' should read 'le capre'). Leonardo also had a pair of trestles. But these he used on top of his platform in the Great Hall rather than to support it. Ibid., p. 134, no. 225; and esp. p. 135, no. 228 (both May-June 1505): 'uno paio di capre a Lionardo da Vinci in sul palchetto' ('a pair of trestles for Leonardo da Vinci on the platform'). The tops of the windows are reported to have been at 6.4m or 11 *braccia*, and the *cornicione* was at between 18 and 19 *braccia* (10.5 and 11.1m); see nn. 7 and 131. On how high the frame for the altarpiece came, see n. 131.

135 Michelangelo normally filled his paintings and sculptural reliefs from top to bottom and side to side with figures, just as we see in the well-known copy after a piece of his cartoon (Fig. 6). The top and bottom of the composition, especially, both clearly seem to follow anticipated borders. If Michelangelo's mural really was to have depicted the Battle of Cascina (fought in 1364) according to the account given by Filippo Villani, as is generally assumed, the completed scene of the *Bathing Soldiers* would not have shown fighting in the background, as is often imagined, for the simple reason that there was no fighting during or immediately after the incident apparently depicted. This action entailed the unprepared Florentine soldiers reacting to a false alarm

raised by an alert commissioner several hours before the battle began, when the enemy was still in Pisa, six miles away. *Cronache di Giovanni, Matteo e Filippo Villani*, Triest, II, 1858, p. 409, col. I.

136 See p. 40 at n. 122. We are assuming that Michelangelo's figures, just like those of Leonardo, were somewhat larger than life-sized. That is how an inventory of 1635 describes the figures in a piece of cartoon in the Royal Palace in Turin which was believed at the time to have been part of Michelangelo's original and has since been destroyed by fire. See C. de Tolnay, *Michelangelo*, Princeton, 1945, I, p. 209.

137 C.-A. Isermeyer, 'Die Arbeiten Leonardos und Michelangelos für den grossen Ratsaal in Florenz', in *Studien zur toskanischen Kunst: Festschrift für Ludwig Heinrich Heydenreich zum 23. März 1963*, ed. W. Lotz and L. L. Möller, Munich, 1964, pp. 83–130, esp. p. 115. Isermeyer's figures for the number of sheets and the size of the paper have been verified by C. Bambach, *Drawing and Painting in the Italian Renaissance Workshop*, Cambridge, 1999, pp. 35–36 and 42; and eadem, 'The Purchases of Cartoon Paper for Leonardo's *Battle of Anghiari* and Michelangelo's *Battle of Cascina*', *I Tatti Studies*, VIII, 1999, pp. 105–33. (In the latter Bambach gives a figure for the area of the usable surface that is slightly greater than the one given here and also proposes, on the strength of very little evidence, that only half of the paper was used for the master cartoon, while the other half was set aside to be used later on to make a duplicate to transfer the design to the wall. If so, one wonders, why were all of Leonardo's other supplies bought only at the time he actually used them, and why was Leonardo given more paper 'per la pictura' ['for the picture'] around the time he was preparing to paint? See p. 44 at n. 139.) 252m$^2$ is the area we obtain if we take the smallest known value for the Bo-

lognese royal folio (438 x 605mm). If we take the largest (452 x 617mm), the area of the paper would have been 265m².

138 The flour is recorded in Frey (as in n. 16), p. 132, no. 177 (May-June 1504). On the hem see the following note. Vasari writes (ed. Milanesi, IV, p. 41), as does Varchi (as in n. 83), that Leonardo *began* his cartoon. Giovanni Bottari flatly states that he did not finish it; see n. 126. The artist's agreement with the *Signoria* allowed him not to finish the cartoon if he started painting instead by the end of February 1505; Frey, pp. 130–31, no. 175 (or Villata [as in n. 1], pp. 166–68, no. 189). He did not start painting during that month, but substantial documentation shows that he did begin soon afterwards to prepare the special surface on which he would paint; Frey, pp. 133–34, passim. He also may have begun around this time to make the trial panel of which the *Codice Magliabechiano* speaks (as in n. 71) and of which we appear to have a copy in a print of 1558 by Lorenzo Zacchia of Lucca. This now lost panel possibly was the 'sagio per la pictura' ('sample for the picture') mentioned in a record of March–April 1505; Frey, p. 134, no. 216. See also Wilde, 'Michelangelo and Leonardo' (as in n. 104), p. 70.

139 We are assuming that the numerous sheets (at least 950 had been supplied; see Frey, p. 129, no. 161 [January-February 1504]) overlapped by 3cm and that 1.5cm were lost under the cloth hem in the cartoon's borders. Three centimeters is the approximate amount of overlap found in Raphael's cartoon in the Pinacoteca Ambrosiana at Milan for the figural part of his *School of Athens* in the *Stanze* of the Vatican Palace, in which comparable strength was needed. The cloth for the hem is documented in Operai di Palazzo, 10, fol. 60v (January-February 1504): 'et per uno lenzuolo et 3 teli, dato a decto Lionardo per orlare el cartone' ('and for a sheet and 3 pieces of cloth

given to the said Leonardo to hem the cartoon'). It cost more than 16½ *lire*—that is, more than the monthly wages of an unskilled laborer. At 11 *soldi* per *braccio* (cf. n. 129) the length of this cloth before cutting would have been just over 30 *braccia* or 17.6m, yielding a hem that must have been very long indeed. If we take the largest known value for the Bolognese royal folio, the cartoon's surface could have been 235m²—or more, if more paper was used than that for which records exist; see n. 137. The paper cost 11 or 12 *soldi* per *quaderno* (25 sheets) or 11 or 12 *lire* per ream (500 sheets; there were 20 *quaderni* to a ream and 20 *soldi* to a *lira*); Frey, p. 129, no. 161; and p. 134, no. 219 (March-April 1505). That price made it one of the most expensive papers available at the time. Paper for normal office use usually cost 3½-5 *lire* per ream (these are the prices given in Camera dell'Arme, 16 [1506], passim).

140 The three *quaderni* were paid for in March or April 1505; Frey, p. 134, no. 219. That Leonardo had already used at least all but one *quaderno* (25 sheets) of the at least 38 *quaderni* (950 sheets) of paper with which he began is evident from the fact that he now received three *quaderni* (75 sheets) more. That he used a duplicate to transfer the part of his cartoon showing the *Capture of a Standard* to the wall is clear from the fact that the master could still be seen in the Palace after Leonardo had abandoned the project; *Codice Magliabechiano* (as in n. 71), p. 111: 'il disegno del gruppo de' cavallj, che hoggi in opera si vede, rimase in Palazo' ('the drawing of the group of the horses, which one today sees realized [in painting], remained in the Palace'). If Leonardo had used the master, it almost certainly would have been badly mutilated during the transfer because of the great stresses the paper had to undergo during this process as well as the damages caused by the moisture, powders, sharp styluses and nails that were used for it. Obviously he had to use a duplicate to transfer the part to be paint-

ed if the master was still in one enormous piece at the time the transfer was made—as it likely was in view of the fact that it was hemmed; see previous note. The cartoon by Raphael in the Pinacoteca Ambrosiana in Milan for the figural part of his *School of Athens* is one example of a beautifully prepared master from which a duplicate was taken. That Leonardo's master cartoon was beautifully drawn as well is clear from some of the materials that were bought for it; see Frey, p. 132, nos. 183–84 (July-August 1504); and p. 133, no. 200 (September-October). An example of what Leonardo was capable of is his matchless *Burlington House Cartoon* in the National Gallery in London. Michelangelo's cartoon also was consummately drawn and 'painted'. See Cellini (as in n. 5); Vasari-Milanesi, VII, p. 160; and Frey, p. 133, no. 208 (January-February 1505): 'per dipignere el cartone'.

141  If Leonardo did not finish his master cartoon by the target date of 28 February 1505 (see n. 138), does that mean that he did not fill all of the available paper, or that he did fill it but still had not prepared the entire battle mural? And did this cartoon correspond to the whole battle mural or only those parts of it containing important groups of figures (as in the case of Raphael's cartoon in Milan for the *School of Athens*)? If Leonardo's master cartoon in fact was at least 223m$^2$ in area, his mural must have been planned to be at least 28.5m long (including at least 0.6m of frame on both sides), as it probably could not have been more than 14 *braccia* or 8.2m high throughout most of its length (see the following note), or 11 *braccia* or 6.4m (19 - 8*br* or 11.1 - 4.7m) high over the *residenza* or tribune of the *Signoria*, which probably was 12 *braccia* or 7.0m wide (see pp. 16 at n. 50; and 22 at n. 73). At least one metre of it would have had to be over the *residenza*. If Leonardo's mural was to have been at least 223m$^2$ in area and also perfectly rectangular, its length would probably have been

at least 36.0m ($223m^2 \div 6.4m + 1.2m$), and Michelangelo's mural could not have fit on the same wall (if we assume that if it was to have been painted there it would have to have been the same size and shape as Leonardo's).

142 The murals could not have greatly exceeded 14 *braccia* or 8.2m in height, as no more wall than that is likely to have been available; the wooden wainscotting or *spalliere* in back of the *ringhiera* probably came to a height of at least 5 *braccia* or 2.9m, and the cornice underneath the ceiling probably rested at a level of no more than 19 *braccia* or 11.1m (Fig. 4). Over the *residenza* of the *Signoria* a mural probably could not have been taller than 6.4m. See p. 22 at n. 72; and p. 25 at n. 81; and the preceding note.

143 See p. 43 at n. 135. For the two rooms in which the cartoons were prepared, see n. 164. One greatly doubts that a cartoon (or piece of cartoon) over 12 *braccia* or 7.0m tall could have been stored or displayed on three thick planks in the (living or storage quarters in the) *ballatoio* or fortified roof area of the Palace, as Michelangelo's was (see n. 157). If we wish to compare what Leonardo and Michelangelo would have produced with the frescoes that Vasari did produce in the same place in the late 1560s and early 1570s, which are 7.5m tall (Fig. 1), we must keep in mind that Vasari worked on walls that are 12 *braccia* or 7.0m (or possibly 13 *braccia* or 7.6m) higher than those on which Leonardo painted and Michelangelo was to have painted *and* that the two earlier artists worked or were to have worked on walls the lower parts of which contained windows (on one side), accommodations for government officials, a 'chapel' and so on. Vasari boasts that his wall panels were the biggest ever: 'i quali spartimenti delle facciate sono tanto grandi che non si sono anco veduti maggiori spazj per fare istorie di pitture né dagli antichi né

dai moderni' ('the which wall panels are so large that bigger spaces for making stories in painting have not yet been seen either by the ancients or by the moderns'); ed. Milanesi, IV, p. 452. It certainly does not sound as if Vasari thought that the murals of Leonardo and Michelangelo were going to have been almost as tall as his.

144 See pp. 47–48 beginning at n. 154; and esp. 50–51 beginning at n. 164. If the two murals were expected to be the same size, why did Leonardo initially receive 950 royal folios of paper and Michelangelo only 350? See Frey (as in n. 16), p. 129, no. 161 (January-February 1504); and p. 133, no. 193 (September-October). Why was it believed that 75 royal folios more would enable Michelangelo to 'finish' (*fornire*) his cartoon—which he clearly did not (see p. 48 at n. 157)? See Frey, p. 133, no. 199 (November-December 1504). Why, finally, did Michelangelo prepare his cartoon using the simplest of scaffolds, whereas Leonardo's clearly was much more elaborate? See the beginning of p. 51. On the possibility that the two murals were nevertheless to have been the same size—or at least the same height—but painted on opposite walls, see p. 51, paragraph following n. 168.

145 In the agreement between Leonardo and the *Signoria*, his mural is called 'un quadro' ('a rectangular panel', 'a painting') as well as 'tal pictura' ('such picture'); Frey (as in n. 16), p. 130, no. 175 (or Villata [as in n. 1], p. 166, no. 189). In true fresco painting the only pigments that should be used are those known as 'earth colours', capable of retaining their colour after prolonged contact with the atmosphere. (Pigments mixed in oil are sealed off by it from the atmosphere.) The pigments are mixed with water and applied to the plaster while it is still wet or 'fresh' (*fresco*) and is still 'taking', and thus become embedded in its surface.

146 For the statue of the *Holy Saviour*, which was not made, see Frey, p. 126, no. 128 (1502).

147 The possible clock, which evidently had an area of somewhat less than 19½ square *braccia* or 6.65m² and also was boarded up, is recorded in Operai di Palazzo, 14, fol. 19r (November 1513): 'A Francesco lengnia[i]uo[lo] detto Francesco di Capello per braccia 19½ d'asse di terzo d'albero per coprire l'oriuolo di Sala ché si difenda dala polvere secondo comandò Giovannj Berardj alora Gonfaloniere —— £4.7' ('To Francesco the woodworker called Francesco di Capello for 19½ *braccia* of boards of poplar of a third [of a *braccio*] to cover the clock of the Hall so it may be defended from the dust as Giovanni Berardi, then Gonfalonier, commanded'). (Previously uncited; Berardi had been Gonfalonier during July and August.) That square rather than linear *braccia* are meant seems clear if we compare the figures given here with those in the record cited in n. 69. We do not know when this clock was made or where it was located. It is possible that the word 'Sala' here refers to the Sala dei Gigli (Hall of the Lilies), the Room of the Gonfalonier, or the Sala dei Dugento (Hall of the Two Hundred) rather than the Great Hall. If this clock indeed was in the Hall, its position there may well have had something to do with the placement of the battle murals.

148 Villata (as in n. 1), p. 203, no. 236: 'un piccolo principio a una opera grande doveva fare' ('a small beginning to a great work he was supposed to make'); and no. 235: 'quale [opera] non è altro non ha incominciato' ('the which [work], moreover, he has not begun').

149 See n. 150.

150 Michelangelo to his brother Buonarroto, 2 July 1508: 'el mio chartone che io chominciai alla Sala' ('my cartoon that I began

for the Hall'); *Carteggio* (as in n. 125), I, 1965, p. 70. Also Piero Soderini (the Gonfalonier of Justice) to the Cardinal of Volterra (his brother), 27 November 1506: 'ha principiato una storia per il pubblico che sarà cosa admiranda' ('he has begun a story [scil., narrative painting] for the public that will be an amazing thing'); Frey (as in n. 16), p. 113, no. 54. In a letter probably written at the end of 1523 Michelangelo would say that he had completed the cartoon (*Carteggio*, III, p. 7). But that is just one of the many misleading or deliberately false statements found in that letter. Vasari says that Michelangelo began the cartoon (in 1504–5), went to Rome, and then finished it in three months after having returned to Florence (in 1506); ed. Milanesi, VII, pp. 160 and 168. But no documentary evidence substantiates this last assertion, which in any case appears to contradict what Soderini wrote to his brother in November 1506 and definitely contradicts what Michelangelo himself wrote to his in 1508. It is probable that Vasari mistook a part of it for Michelangelo's entire cartoon, as he evidently did in the case of Leonardo's; see n. 83. According to Ascanio Condivi (*Vita di Michelagnolo Buonarroti*, ed. G. Nencioni, intr. M. Hirst and C. Elam, Florence, 1998, p. 25), Michelangelo's cartoon (was to have) represented 'la guerra tra Fiorenza e Pisa e i molti e vari accidenti occorsi in essa' ('the war between Florence and Pisa and the many and varied incidents that occurred in it'). He unfortunately does not say *which* war between Florence and Pisa.

151 The scene of the *Bathing Soldiers* possibly was to have been positioned across from the one by Leonardo often referred to as the *Cavalcade* (Fig. 7), which shows some reserve troops about to go into action and also no doubt was to have been an opener (see p. 37 at n. 113; and n. 120). In fact Wilde, believing that the two scenes were to have been at opposite ends of the same wall, thinks that Michelangelo designed

the *Bathing Soldiers* to 'correspond in reverse' to Leonardo's *Cavalcade*; 'Michelangelo and Leonardo' (as in n. 104), p. 74.

152 Vasari-Milanesi, IV, pp. 198–99. The title given here for the painting is derived from the words used in Deliberazioni, 131 (1529), fol. 58r; see n. 21.

153 Piero de' Medici had been expelled from Florence on the Day of the Holy Saviour (9 November) 1494; it was therefore imagined that Jesus himself had actively intervened to help drive him out. A statue of the Holy Saviour (by Andrea Sansovino) was to have been placed over the head of the Gonfalonier of Justice on top of the *residenza* of the *Signoria* and thus probably either at the bottom of or else underneath the battle mural by Leonardo; Frey (as in n. 16), p. 126, no. 128 (1502). The Florentines invoked the help of Mary (along with that of Jesus and St John the Baptist) when they founded their own army in December 1506 (before then they had always used foreign mercenaries); Provvisioni, 197 (bobina 378), fols. 34r–39v. A 'deliberation' passed by the *Signori e Collegi* in November 1529 required all Florentines unable to fight to kneel and pray for victory to Christ and the Virgin for the duration of all battles fought by the Florentine armies; an 'Ave Maria' sounded by the great bell of the Palace (probably the same bell that summoned the councilmen to Council) would notify the city of the beginning of these battles; Deliberazioni, 132, fol. 4r–v. That the Council had been ordained by God was affirmed in one of the Hall's inscriptions or 'epitaphs'; Landucci (as in n. 16), p. 126. There was a monogram of Jesus on the curtain of Fra Bartolomeo's unfinished altarpiece, which curtain was made in May and decorated in June 1529; Camera dell'Arme, 31, fols. 40r and 43r; and Frey, p. 136, no. 256.

154　Examples include the frescoes in the Sala del Mappamondo (Council Hall) in the Palazzo Pubblico in Siena; the murals by Pisanello in the Ducal Palace in Mantua; the *Battle of San Romano* panels by Paolo Uccello in the Uffizi in Florence, the Louvre in Paris, and the National Gallery in London; and the frescoes by Giulio Romano in the Sala di Costantino in the Vatican Palace. The placement of the battle frescoes by Vasari now in the Great Hall does not apply, as Vasari quite unusually put numerous windows at the tops of its side walls; his frescoes do come to just below these windows (Fig. 1). We are not counting the battle scenes found in religious cycles such as those representing subjects from the Old Testament, the lives of certain saints, or the Legend of the True Cross, as the position of such scenes usually depends on where the battles they depict occur in the narrative.

155　For the distance from the *residenza* to the cornice, see n. 141. On the scene's being low in the mural as well as probably not having been planned to have anything important over it, see p. 21. It is possible, to be sure, that the mural was to have been taller where the *Capture* is or was than it was in the centre. That is, it is possible that the mural was to have surrounded or 'enframed' the upper part of the *residenza* rather than been perfectly rectangular.

156　Frey (as in n. 16), p. 129, no. 161 (January-February 1504): 'ebbe Lionardo da Vincio per fare el cartone alla Sala' ('received by Leonardo da Vinci to make the cartoon for the Hall'). See also nn. 140 and 141.

157　See n. 150. During the first two months of 1505, 4 lbs of tacks (*tozetti*) were bought for one of the cartoons; Operai di Palazzo, 10, fol. 75r (previously uncited). One suspects that the cartoon in question was Michelangelo's and that the tacks were used to mount it, or part of it, on a frame or stretcher. In July or August of the same year, Michelangelo's cartoon was placed—obviously in some protected place—on three 'panchoncelli' (thick planks) in the *ballatoio* (fortified roof area) of the Palace, where the quarters of the Gonfalonier of Justice and his wife had just been built a few years earlier; Frey, p. 135, no. 234.

158 In all Michelangelo is recorded to have received 17 *quaderni* or 425 sheets; Frey, p. 133, nos. 193 (September-October 1504) and 198 (November-December). For the size of these sheets see n. 137. That Michelangelo used or started to use all, or nearly all, of the at least 113m² is highly likely, as the last 3 *quaderni* (75 sheets) were bought 'per fornire el cartone' ('to finish the cartoon'). The amount of sifted flour used to paste Michelangelo's cartoon (the pasting took at least 10½ *opere* or workdays) evidently was but a fraction of the amount used to paste Leonardo's; Frey, p. 133, nos. 194 (September-October 1504) and 202 (November-December); and Operai di Palazzo, 10, fol. 70ʳ (September-October 1504): 'per un quarto e mezo di farina stacciata per inpastare il cartone che fa Michelagnolo . . . £1 ß13' ('for a *quarto* and a half of sifted flour to paste the cartoon that Michelangelo is making . . . £1 s. 13'; previously uncited). One *quarto* (one fourth of a *staio*) and a half amounted to about 9.1 litres or no more than 6.8kg of sifted flour. The recorded flour for Leonardo's cartoon weighed 88 Florentine lbs or 29.9kg; Frey, p. 132, no. 177 (May-June 1504).

159 The figure that results when we divide 100m² by 4.7m (8 *braccia*), that is, the greatest probable height from the tops of the windows and the frame for the altarpiece to the cornice under the ceiling, is 22.2m. Each of the cycles of narrative pictures or 'stories' on the side walls of the Sistine Chapel spans about 40m (including the frames). With the now lost continuations on the end walls, both cycles once covered a distance of

around 53.3m. That Michelangelo's cartoon probably was to have been larger than what could be produced with the 113m² or slightly more of paper that the *Operai* are known to have bought for him is evident from two facts: (1) Michelangelo clearly used or started to use most if not all of the paper he received (see the preceding note); and (2) three and a half years later Michelangelo described the cartoon as 'my cartoon that I began for the Hall' (see n. 150). A *predella* in our sense is the long and very low sequence of (usually framed) pictures that often is or used to be found under the great altar paintings of the fourteenth and fifteenth centuries.

160  On the likelihood that some kind of decoration was to have filled the spaces between and at the sides of the windows, see this page at n. 159; and the end of p. 53.

161  If Michelangelo was not planning to use any internal frames, the lengths would have been around 27.6 and 45.2m and, in the case of scenes of alternating width (see text following), 36.4 and 49.6m respectively. A cartoon corresponding to a mural of this last length would have had an area of around 223m²—at least very nearly the same area that Leonardo's cartoon may have had.

162  That Michelangelo was preparing narrow or squarish scenes as well as wide ones seems quite possible. In the Ashmolean Museum at Oxford there is a drawing by him (no. 294) of a scene remarkably like the action group at the right side of Raphael's *Punishment of Heliodorus* in the *Stanze* in the Vatican, in which the pose of the Heliodorus is almost identical to that of the Paul in Michelangelo's *Conversion of St Paul* in the Pauline Chapel, also in the Vatican. Raphael is known to have borrowed a great deal from Michelangelo's cartoon, and Michelangelo often recycled his poses. But as far as we know he *never* copied from Raphael. It thus appears that something like the

scene in Michelangelo's drawing (and the group in Raphael's painting) once existed, probably incompletely, in those parts of Michelangelo's battle cartoon whose contents are now unknown. That other parts or pieces of the cartoon once existed seems clear from the following phrase in Francesco Albertini's *Memoriale* of 1510 (as in n. 100): '(Nella Sala Grande Nuova del Consiglio Maiore) . . . li disegni di Michelangelo' ('[In the Great New Hall of the Major Council] . . . the drawings of Michelangelo'); as well as from a comparison of the probable area of the *Bathing Soldiers* section (around $39.6m^2$) with the useful area of the paper Michelangelo is known to have received and at least mostly used (around $100m^2$).

163 The important surviving battle paintings of the period usually run or ran the full length of the walls on which they are or were painted or mounted. Examples are the same as those listed in n. 154, with the possible exception of the Paolo Uccello's *Battle of San Romano*. (We obviously are not counting Vasari's frescoes in the Hall, which could not run the full length of its walls because of the *Udienza* [Fig. 1, middle], or battle scenes in religious cycles and so on.)

164 For these spaces, neither of which survives, see W. and E. Paatz, *Die Kirchen von Florenz*, Frankfort, 1952-55, III, pp. 671–72, 676, 699 and 755; and IV, p. 460. According to Marco Lastri (*L'osservatore fiorentino sugli edifizi della sua patria*, 3rd edn, Florence, 1821, III, p. 135) the Sala del Papa measured 138 x 23 *braccia* (80.6 x 13.4m), that is, the full length and width of the upper floor of the west wing of the Great Cloister of Santa Maria Novella. (For its height he gives the unlikely figure of 22 *braccia* or 12.85m.) But according to the diarist Landucci the Sala del Papa was not a single room but a suite of rooms. And in fact the church historian Giuseppe Richa writes (*Notizie istoriche delle chiese fiorentine . . .*, Florence, 1754-62 [Rome,

1972], III, p. 117) that the upper floor of the west wing of the Great Cloister of Santa Maria Novella contained three spaces, each 23 *braccia* wide: a vestibule of 12 *braccia* (7.0m); a very large room, which he calls the Great Hall of the (Ecumenical) Council (of 1439), 84 *braccia* (49.0m) long; and another large room, which he calls the Sala del Papa, 42 *braccia* (24,5m) long. (My thanks to Kelley Magill for this information.) If this area in fact was configured as Richa says, Leonardo's cartoon perhaps was no longer than 49.0m and in that case did not run the full length of the east wall of the Great Hall. (It probably would have been at least 4.55m tall in that case.) However the upper floor of the west wing of the Great Cloister of Santa Maria Novella may have been configured, the Sala del Papa, with which a large stable was associated, was an impressive room or suite of rooms. Anton Francesco Doni reports the performance of two plays there (*I Marmi*, ed. E. Chiorboli, Bari, 1928, I, p. 51). Other evidence of the Sala's great size is found in Operai di Palazzo, 14 (1513–23), passim. See also nn. 18 and 165; as well as Frey (as in n. 16), p. 129, no. 166; and p. 130, no. 170 (both January-February 1504). Local historians assure me that the Sala dei Tintori was a very large room also.

165 Frey, p. 129, no. 161 (January-February 1504); p. 133, nos. 193 and 198 (September-October and November-December); and p. 134, no. 219 (March-April 1505). Leonardo's paper cost 11 or 12 *soldi* per *quaderno* (25 sheets); Michelangelo's cost 10. The paper Leonardo used for his cartoon also was slightly more expensive than the 53–56m$^2$ of royal folios he used to fill the 'finestre salvatiche' (literally: 'wild windows') of the room in which he prepared it, which cost 10 *soldi* and 4 *denari* (there were 12 *denari* to a *soldo*) per *quaderno*; Frey, p. 129, no. 164 (January-February 1504). These 'finestre salvatiche' must have been temporary windows made to compensate for the other windows, having an area of perhaps around

45m², that Leonardo had caused to be covered or filled with boards costing around 25 *lire*, presumably so he could position his cartoon over them; ibid., no. 166 (same date). On the sifted flour with which the paste was made, see n. 158.

166 See n. 134; and Frey, p. 133, no. 199 (November-December 1504).

167 Sometimes a ladder is mentioned in connexion with it. See Frey, p. 129, no. 166; p. 130, nos. 167, 169 and 172 (all January-February 1504); and p. 132, nos. 181–82 (July-August). The various items concerning the construction of the *ponte* added up to perhaps 80–100 *lire*. In spite of what Vasari relates (ed. Milanesi, IV, pp. 42–43), there appears to have been nothing unusual about either of Leonardo's *ponti*, except that the platform of the one in the Hall must have been cantilevered in such a way as to project over the *ringhiera*, which had a reported depth of three *braccia*, or 1.75m. It even may also have projected over the *residenza* of the *Signoria*, which probably was deeper, especially where the *aliette* or 'little wings' were (on them see n. 63). But it is possible that this *ponte* did not permit Leonardo to work right away over the *residenza*, and that could be the reason why he began his mural over the Twelve Good Men rather than the *Signoria*. Leonardo did not himself make the *ponte* that he used in the Hall; Frey, p. 133, no. 209 (January-February 1505): 'A Giovanni d'Andrea piffero (*Benvenuto Cellini's father*) per haver fatto fare el ponte a Lionardo da Vinci' ('To Giovanni d'Andrea the piper for having had the scaffolding made for Leonardo da Vinci').

168 See pp. 22–23 after n. 73; and 42 at n. 130. The height of the walls up to the cornice was between 10.5 and 11.1m; see nn. 7 and 81.

169 See p. 44 at n. 138.

170 See n. 141.

171  See also n. 161.

172  If the *Capture* can be shown to begin or have begun below around 6.8m, the two murals evidently were to have been different.  If it begins or began above that level, they probably were to have been the same, at least in height.  The height of Leonardo's full mural should correspond to that of his specially prepared surface, of which—if it has survived—there ought to be a good deal; see n. 99.

173  We are assuming that there originally was no bare wall underneath the *Last Supper*.  (In the nineteenth century there definitely was none.)  The wall above it was fully decorated, as was the wall at the opposite end of the refectory containing the large fresco of the *Crucifixion* by Montorfano (except for a very low area at the bottom, where woodwork no doubt used to be).

174  Cerretani (as in n. 1), p. 116: 'cominc[i]ò a dipignere la Sala del Consiglio' ('began to paint the Hall of the Council'); Michelangelo (*Carteggio* [as in n. 125], III, p. 7): 'io avevo tolto a fare la metà della Sala del Consiglio' ('I had undertaken to do half of the Hall of the Council'); Vasari (ed. Milanesi, IV, p. 41): gli [scil., a Lionardo] fu allogata la detta Sala' ('the said Hall was assigned to him [scil., Leonardo]'); and (VII, p. 159): 'onde fu cagione che egli [scil., Michelagnolo] facesse a concorrenza di Lionardo l'altra facciata' ('whence it came about that he [scil., Michelangelo] might do the other wall in competition with Leonardo').

175  Frey (as in n. 16), p. 130, no. 175 (or Villata [as in n. 1], p. 166, no. 189).

176  Charles of Amboise on Leonardo: 'uno homo de tanta virtute' ('a man of such ability'); Villata, p. 204, no. 237.  Soderini

on Leonardo's mural: 'una opera grande doveva fare' ('a great work he was supposed to make'); ibid., p. 203, no. 236; on Michelangelo: 'nel mestieri suo [*sculpture*] è unico in Italia—forse etiam in universo' ('in his trade [*sculpture*] he is unique in Italy—perhaps even in the world'); and: 'luj farà cose che si maraviglierà chi le vedrà' ('he will do things that whoever sees them will be amazed'); and on Michelangelo's mural: 'sarà cosa admiranda' ('it will be an amazing thing'); Frey, p. 113, no. 54. Cerretani (as in n. 1) on Leonardo: 'maestro grandissimo . . . di pittura' ('a very great master . . . of painting'); and on the two artists (p. 212 [September-October 1509]): 'In questi tempi era duo fiorentini primarii ed ecelentti in ischoltura et pitura, l'uno de' quali si chiamava Lionardo di ser Piero da Vinci; non era legiptimo . . . lavorava pocho. L'altro era Michelagnolo di Francesco di Bonaroto Simoni ciptadino [*sic*] . . . lavorava più e bene . . .' ('In these times there were two Florentines who were foremost and excellent in sculpture and painting, one of whom was called Leonardo di Ser Piero da Vinci; he was not legitimate . . . he worked little. The other was the citizen Michelangelo di Francesco di Buonarroto Simoni [*sic*] . . . he worked more and well . . .') Varchi (as in n. 83) on the two artists: 'onde Michelagnolo per vincere colui [scil., Leonardo], il qual vinceva di gran lunga tutti gl'Altri . . .' ('wherefore Michelangelo, in order to defeat him [scil., Leonardo], who defeated by far all the Others . . .').

# INDEX

# THE FLORENTINE

*The Florentine* is a bi-weekly newspaper for the English-speaking community of Florence, including residents, students, visiting professionals, and tourists. With an international editorial staff and over 200 contributing writers from around the globe, it is the most widely read English paper in Florence and reaches subscribers world-wide.

Serving online subscribers to *The Florentine*, www.theflorentine.net also features the current issue of the paper and upcoming events in and around Florence, as well as a photo repository, blogs, and back issues and an archive of articles from the paper.

The Florentine Press is dedicated to publishing books in English about Florence and Italy, both past and present. From essays to scholarly studies, the books from The Florentine Press explore this rich and vibrant culture, its language, food and wine, arts, history, and terrain. Current titles are available in bookstores in Italy and the United States, and through www.theflorentine.net:

*Finding Leonardo: The Case for Recovering the 'Battle of Anghiari'*, by Rab Hatfield

*Italians Dance and I'm a Wallflower: Adventures in Italian Expression,* by Linda Falcone
(also available through Amazon.com as *Italian, It's All Greek to Me: Everything You Need to Know About Italian Language and Culture,* by Linda Falcone and Leo Cardini)

The Florentine
via dei Banchi, 4
50123 Florence
phone +39.055.2306616 • fax +39.055.9060996
info@theflorentine.net • www.theflorentine.net

Creative group Agile Logica (www. agilelogica.it) designs *The Florentine*, www.theflorentine.net, and the books of The Florentine Press.

*Notes*

*Notes*

*Notes*

*Notes*